# COOKING FOR
# *EVERYONE*

# COOKING FOR
# EVERYONE

EBURY PRESS · LONDON

*Clover is a Registered Trademark of Dairy Crest Limited*

*Published by Ebury Press*
*an imprint of Century Hutchinson Ltd*
*Brookmount House*
*62–65 Chandos Place*
*London WC2N 4NW*

*ISBN 0 85223 826 6*

*Editor: Carole McGlynn*
*Designer: Grahame Dudley Associates*
*Photographer: James Murphy*
*Home Economists: Janet Smith, Emma-lee Gow, Allyson Birch*
*Stylists: Kay McGlone, Sarah Wiley*
*Illustrator: Lesley Champkins*

*Filmset by Advanced Filmsetters (Glasgow) Ltd*
*Printed and bound in Italy by New Interlitho S.p.a., Milan*

**Cookery Notes**

1 *Follow either metric or imperial measures for the recipes in this book as they are not interchangeable.*

2 *All spoon measures are level unless otherwise stated.*

3 *Sets of measuring spoons are available in both metric and imperial size to give accurate measurement of small quantities.*

4 *When measuring milk, the exact conversion of 568 ml (1 pint) has been used.*

5 *Size 4 and 3 eggs should be used except where otherwise stated.*

6 *Plain or self-raising flour can be used unless otherwise stated. Use white, brown or wholemeal flour according to your preference.*

7 *Brown or white breadcrumbs can be used unless otherwise stated.*

# Contents

Introduction 6

Soups & Starters 9

Light Meals & Snacks 19

Meat 29

Chicken & Poultry 42

Fish & Seafood 54

Accompaniments 64

Desserts 71

Baking 84

Index 95

# INTRODUCTION

**Clover® Cooking for Everyone** has been put together with different families' tastes and ways of life in mind. It is full of recipes and ideas from everyday meals with the children, to special menus with friends.

Clover is a buttery tasting spread made from fresh cream and vegetable oil. It has a delicious taste like butter with the real convenience of spreadability, even straight from the fridge.

Clover can be used in exactly the same way as butter: it can be melted, creamed, spread, diced, rubbed-in and even used for frying.

If you are in a hurry, there is no need to wait for Clover to soften. Its spreadability means that it is always ready to use on sandwiches and quick snacks and for cooking, saving you the extra time and effort needed when you are using hard butter.

Clover stores well too. It keeps in the refrigerator for up to three weeks, and in the freezer for three months. When frozen, allow it to defrost slowly in the fridge and do not re-freeze.

Above all, it is Clover's taste that makes people use it. The flavour proves that you really can have all the taste plus convenience that today's cooks demand.

And if you prefer the mild taste of pale continental butters, try Clover Slightly Salted instead. It has a creamy flavour like butter from France and Germany with all the cooking, freezing and spreading properties of Clover.

## MEAL PLANNING

This book provides a useful source of recipes for family needs, quick midweek suppers or something special for a family occasion or entertaining.

*Mixed Fruit Teabread (page 94)*

Everyone needs inspiration from time to time, and this book provides interesting and different ideas that you know will work as they have been double tested in an internationally renowned test kitchen.

When planning a meal choose a range of dishes that will give a variety of colours, textures and flavours. Seafood and vegetable dishes are popular as starters with main courses of fish or meat dishes accompanied by lightly cooked fresh vegetables, pasta, rice or salad. Your choice of dessert will depend on what has gone before. If the main course has been quite filling then a light dessert will round off the meal perfectly. If, however, you have decided on a light main course, then you can afford to indulge in a rich dessert.

The other very important factor in planning a meal is time. To help you plan ahead we have included preparation times as well as cooking times in **Clover Cooking for Everyone**.

For light meals and snacks, the relevant chapter is full of delicious ideas. You will also find that some of the soups and accompaniments make a filling light meal, perhaps a Haddock and Corn Chowder.

Some of the recipes are bound to be popular with children, such as Macaroni Pie and Pizza Casalinga which can be made quickly. There are also quite a few biscuits that young mouths will enjoy.

Entertaining and special family occasions are made simple too, with a list of ideas for soups and starters, meat, poultry and fish dishes and very tempting desserts. Many of these recipes can be prepared well in advance so that you can relax and socialise with everyone else.

The chapter on accompaniments provides you with an inspiring change to peas and carrots!

The dessert section includes hot and cold dishes. For entertaining, Baked Alaska never fails to impress, but if you want to prepare something in advance a Raspberry Walnut Torte is delicious.

All of the chapters have some new and tempting ideas to try. Stilton Steaks combine contrasting flavours, or Parsley Chicken with Cashews gives a new crunchy texture to chicken. There are some old favourites as well, like Liver and Bacon with Potato Pancakes, and Bread and Butter Pudding.

Finally the baking chapter is full of delicious ideas for the tea table from muesli biscuits to the indulgent Hot Chocolate Cheesecake. Clover is used in the baking as well as spreading on teabread—a real all-rounder.

All in all, this book is packed full of delicious recipes to keep the family happy, or to serve to guests on a special occasion. You are bound to turn to it again and again for recipe ideas or to learn how to make the best use of Clover. You will soon discover the many different ways in which Clover can help cut corners in food preparation, whether you are making a complete meal, baking a cake, or simply putting together a quick round of sandwiches, and you can be sure that whatever you make will have a rich and creamy flavour like butter.

# Chapter 1

# Soups & Starters

# CURRIED PARSNIP AND APPLE SOUP

**SERVES 4**
*Preparation time: 30 minutes*
*Cooking time: 50 minutes*

| |
|---|
| 550 g (1¼ lb) parsnips, peeled and sliced |
| 350 g (12 oz) cooking apples, peeled and sliced |
| 40 g (1½ oz) butter or Clover |
| 15 ml (1 tbsp) light oil |
| 15 ml (1 tbsp) mild curry powder |
| 350 g (12 oz) leeks, washed and sliced |
| 1.1 litres (2 pints) chicken stock |
| 300 ml (10 fl oz) milk |
| 150 ml (5 fl oz) dry white wine |
| salt and pepper |
| green apple slices, to garnish |

**1** Heat butter or Clover and oil in a large saucepan. Add curry powder, leeks, parsnips and cooking apples. Stir well to mix, cover and cook gently for 10–15 minutes, or until the vegetables are soft but not coloured.

**2** Pour in the stock, milk and wine. Bring to the boil, cover and simmer gently for 25–30 minutes.

**3** Purée in a food processor or blender until quite smooth. Reheat, adjusting seasoning as necessary. Garnish with apple slices to serve.

# CHICKEN WATERZOOI

**SERVES 6**
*Preparation time: 20 minutes*
*Cooking time: 1 hour 45 minutes*

| |
|---|
| 1.4 kg (3 lb) chicken or boiling fowl, with giblets |
| ½ lemon |
| 2 sticks of celery, chopped |
| 2 leeks, trimmed and chopped |
| 1 medium onion, skinned and chopped |
| 2 carrots, peeled and sliced |
| 1 bouquet garni |
| salt and pepper |
| ½ bottle dry white wine |
| 2 egg yolks |
| 90 ml (6 tbsp) single cream |
| 30 ml (2 tbsp) chopped fresh parsley |

**1** Prick the chicken all over with a skewer, then rub with the cut lemon, squeezing the fruit as you do so to release the juice.

**2** Put the chicken in a large saucepan with the giblets, vegetables, bouquet garni and salt and pepper to taste. Pour in the wine, then add enough water to just cover the chicken.

**3** Bring the liquid to the boil, then lower the heat and half cover with a lid. Simmer for 1½ hours, or until the meat is tender and beginning to fall away from the bones.

**4** Remove the chicken from the liquid. Discard the bouquet garni and the giblets. Cut the chicken flesh into bite-sized pieces, discarding all skin and bones, then return to the liquid.

**5** Mix together the egg yolks and cream in a heatproof bowl. Stir in a few ladlefuls of the hot cooking liquid.

**6** Return this mixture to the pan. Simmer until thickened, stirring constantly, then add the parsley. Taste and adjust seasoning. Serve hot in a warmed soup tureen.

*Right: Chicken Waterzooi*

# MINESTRONE

**SERVES 8**
*Preparation time: 35 minutes*
*Cooking time: 1 hour 10 minutes*

| |
|---|
| 60 ml (4 tbsp) olive oil |
| 25 g (1 oz) butter or Clover |
| 1 large onion, skinned and chopped |
| 1 clove garlic, skinned and crushed |
| 3 sticks celery |
| 3 carrots |
| 2 large courgettes |
| 450 g (1 lb) tomatoes, skinned, or 400 g (14 oz) can tomatoes |
| 75 g (3 oz) fennel |
| 100 g (4 oz) French or runner beans |
| 100 g (4 oz) green cabbage |
| 1.7 litres (3 pints) beef stock |
| salt and pepper |
| 120 ml (8 tbsp) chopped fresh parsley |
| 400 g (14 oz) can cannellini beans |
| freshly grated Parmesan cheese |

**1** Heat the oil and butter or Clover in a large flame-proof casserole or saucepan. Add the onion and crushed garlic and cook until soft and beginning to turn a golden colour.

**2** Finely chop the remaining vegetables, adding them to the saucepan as they are chopped; stir well to mix. The first vegetables will begin to soften as the remainder are being prepared.

**3** Add the stock, seasoning and parsley. Bring to the boil, cover and simmer very gently for about 45 minutes, or until all the vegetables are nearly tender.

**4** Stir in the drained cannellini beans and simmer for 15 minutes. Season. Serve sprinkled with grated Parmesan.

# CREAM OF WATERCRESS AND CHEESE SOUP

**SERVES 4**
*Preparation time: 35 minutes*
*Cooking time: 20 minutes*

| |
|---|
| 1.1 litres (2 pints) milk |
| slices of carrot and onion, bay leaf, blade of mace and whole black peppercorns for flavouring |
| 50 g (2 oz) butter or Clover |
| 1 large onion, skinned and chopped |
| 1 bunch watercress, chopped |
| 40 g (1½ oz) plain flour |
| salt and pepper |
| 75–100 g (3–4 oz) white Cheshire or Caerphilly cheese, finely grated |

**1** Place the milk and flavouring ingredients in a saucepan. Bring to scalding point, cover and leave to infuse for about 20 minutes.

**2** Melt the butter or Clover in a medium saucepan. Add the vegetables, cover and cook gently for about 10 minutes or until soft but not coloured.

**3** Mix in the flour; cook for 1 minute. Gradually add the strained milk and seasoning. Bring to the boil, stirring constantly, leave uncovered and simmer very gently for 7–10 minutes.

**4** Lightly purée the soup in a blender or food processor; don't overprocess as you want a speckled appearance.

**5** Return to the rinsed-out saucepan; add the cheese. Reheat gently and adjust seasoning.

# ITALIAN SEAFOOD SALAD

**SERVES 6**
*Preparation time: 45 minutes plus 2 hours chilling*
*Cooking time: 30 minutes*

| |
|---|
| *1.1 litres (2 pints) fresh mussels, cleaned and cooked, with cooking liquor reserved* |
| *2.8 litres (5 pints) water* |
| *1 onion, skinned and roughly chopped* |
| *1 bay leaf* |
| *salt and pepper* |
| *350 g (12 oz) squid, cleaned* |
| *350 g (12 oz) shelled scallops* |
| *350 g (12 oz) cooked peeled prawns* |
| *1 small green pepper, cored, seeded and finely sliced into strips* |
| *1 small red pepper, cored, seeded and finely sliced into strips* |
| *1 carrot, peeled* |
| *150 ml (¼ pint) olive oil* |
| *60 ml (4 tbsp) lemon juice* |
| *30 ml (2 tbsp) capers* |
| *45 ml (3 tbsp) chopped fresh parsley* |
| *1 clove garlic, skinned and crushed* |
| *black olives, to garnish* |

**1** In a large saucepan, mix together the cooking liquor from the mussels and 1.75 litres (3 pints) of the measured water. Add the onion, bay leaf and a pinch of salt and bring to the boil. Add the squid and simmer gently for 20 minutes or until tender.

**2** Remove the squid and set aside.

**3** Bring the liquid back to the boil, add the scallops and poach gently for 3 minutes. Remove the scallops from the liquid with a slotted spoon and set aside.

**4** Using a sharp knife, cut the squid into rings approximately 1 cm (½ inch) wide.

**5** Cut the scallops into four, removing the tough muscle (found near the coral or roe).

**6** Reserve a few mussels in their shells for the garnish. Remove the shells from the remaining mussels and put the mussels in a large serving bowl with the squid, prawns and scallops. Add the sliced peppers.

**7** With a potato peeler, shred the carrot into ribbons and add this to the seafood.

**8** Make the dressing. Mix together the oil, lemon juice, capers, parsley and garlic—with pepper to taste. Pour over the seafood. Mix lightly but thoroughly. Taste and add salt if necessary.

**9** Chill for at least 2 hours and then serve garnished with black olives and the reserved mussels in their shells.

# PRAWN AND ARTICHOKE SALAD

**SERVES 3–4**
*Preparation time: 35 minutes*

| |
|---|
| *450 g (1 lb) large Jerusalem artichokes, peeled and cut into julienne strips* |
| *salt and pepper* |
| *lemon juice* |
| *2 limes* |
| *60 ml (4 tbsp) vegetable oil* |
| *20 ml (4 tsp) white wine vinegar* |
| *2.5 ml (½ tsp) wholegrain mustard* |
| *100 g (4 oz) cooked peeled prawns* |
| *25 g (1 oz) toasted flaked almonds* |

**1** Cook the artichoke strips in boiling salted water with lemon juice for 1½–2 minutes only. Drain and cool quickly under cold water.

**2** Pare the rind from the limes and cut into fine needle shreds. Blanch in boiling water; drain.

**3** Whisk together the oil, vinegar, mustard and seasoning, then carefully stir in the cooled artichoke strips with the prawns. Sprinkle over the almonds and lime shreds for serving.

*Left:  Minestrone (page 12)*
*Right:  Haddock and Corn Chowder (page 16)*

# Haddock and Corn Chowder

**SERVES 4–6**
*Preparation time: 25 minutes*
*Cooking time: 30 minutes*

| |
|---|
| 25–50 g (1–2 oz) butter or Clover |
| 450 g (1 lb) old potatoes, peeled and cut into 1 cm (½ inch) dice |
| 2 medium onions, thinly sliced |
| 2.5 ml (½ tsp) chilli powder |
| 600 ml (1 pint) fish or vegetable stock |
| 568 ml (1 pint) milk |
| salt and pepper |
| 225 g (8 oz) fresh haddock fillet |
| 225 g (8 oz) smoked haddock fillet |
| 298 g (10½ oz) can cream-style sweetcorn |
| 100 g (4 oz) peeled prawns |
| chopped fresh parsley |

**1** Heat the butter or Clover in a large saucepan. Add the vegetables and the chilli powder and stir the mixture over a moderate heat for 2–3 minutes.

**2** Pour in the stock and milk with a little seasoning. Bring to the boil, cover and simmer for 10 minutes.

**3** Meanwhile, skin the smoked and fresh haddock fillets and then divide the flesh into fork-sized pieces, discarding all the bones.

**4** Add the haddock to the pan with the corn. Bring back to the boil, cover and simmer until the potatoes are tender and the fish begins to flake apart. Skim.

**5** Stir in the prawns with plenty of parsley. Adjust seasoning. Serve.

# Asparagus Tartlets

**SERVES 8**
*Preparation time: 20 minutes plus 1 hour chilling*
*Cooking time: 25 minutes*

| |
|---|
| 50 g (2 oz) butter or Clover |
| 100 g (4 oz) plain flour |
| 5 ml (1 tsp) Dijon mustard |
| 450 g (1 lb) asparagus spears |
| salt and pepper |
| 30 ml (2 tbsp) sesame seeds |
| 90 ml (6 tbsp) olive oil |
| 45 ml (3 tbsp) vegetable oil |
| 45 ml (3 tbsp) lemon juice |
| endive, to garnish |

**1** Cut or rub the butter or Clover into the flour until evenly blended. Mix the mustard with 25 ml (5 tsp) water. Add to the flour and bind to a firm dough, kneading lightly until just smooth. Chill the pastry.

**2** Roll out the dough and use to line about 8 patty tins. Bake blind until golden brown and well dried out. Remove from the tins and cool.

**3** Cut the heads off the asparagus spears so that they are about 5 cm (2 inches) long. Thinly slice a further 5 cm (2 inches) off each stem—use the remainder for a soup later. Cook the heads and sliced asparagus in boiling salted water for about 4 minutes, or until *just* tender. Drain.

**4** Meanwhile, toast the sesame seeds until they are golden. Whisk together with the oils, lemon juice and seasoning; stir in the warm asparagus and allow to cool, then cover and refrigerate.

**5** Spoon the asparagus into the tartlet cases 30 minutes before serving. Serve garnished with endive.

16

# BAKED AVOCADOS AND MUSHROOMS

**SERVES 4**
*Preparation time: 25 minutes*
*Cooking time: 15 minutes*

50 g (2 oz) butter or Clover
75 g (3 oz) button mushrooms, quartered
1 clove garlic, crushed
45 ml (3 tbsp) chopped fresh parsley
2 small ripe avocados
15 ml (1 tbsp) lemon juice
salt and pepper
60 ml (4 tbsp) fresh brown breadcrumbs
green salad and crusty bread to accompany

**1** Melt the butter or Clover in a small saucepan. Add the mushrooms and garlic. Cook over a gentle heat for 3–4 minutes, or until the mushrooms soften. Stir in parsley. Divide the mushrooms between 4 ramekin dishes with half the butter or Clover.

**2** Peel and dice the avocados; add to the ramekins with lemon juice and seasoning. Sprinkle 15 ml (1 tbsp) breadcrumbs over each ramekin and top with the remaining butter or Clover.

**3** Bake at 200°C (400°F) mark 6 for about 12 minutes, or until really hot. Serve immediately with a crisp green salad and plenty of crusty bread.

# SMOKED TROUT AND APPLE MOUSSE

**SERVES 6**
*Preparation time: 35 minutes plus 3 hours chilling*
*Cooking time: 5 minutes*

2 whole smoked trout, about 350 g (12 oz) total weight
300 g (10 oz) soft cheese
60 ml (4 tbsp) lemon juice
150 g (5 oz) carton natural Greek yogurt
2 small tart eating apples
75 g (3 oz) butter or Clover
5 ml (1 tsp) powdered gelatine
pepper
75 g (3 oz) streaky bacon
chives, to garnish
Melba toast, to serve

**1** Remove the heads, skin and bones from the trout. There should be about 225 g (8 oz) flesh. Place in a liquidiser or food processor with the soft cheese, lemon juice and yogurt.

**2** Peel, core and roughly chop 1 apple into a small saucepan. Add the butter or Clover and cook, stirring, over a low heat until the apple softens; cool slightly. Add to the trout mixture and purée until smooth.

**3** In a small bowl, sprinkle the gelatine over 15 ml (1 tbsp) water. Allow to soak for 2–3 minutes. Heat gently in a pan of simmering water until completely dissolved. Stir into the trout mixture and season with pepper. Spoon into a deep dish, cover with cling film and refrigerate for about 3 hours to set.

**4** Grill the bacon until very crisp. Drain well on absorbent kitchen paper, then crush.

**5** To serve, spoon the trout mousse on to serving plates and sprinkle with the crushed bacon. Garnish with slices of the remaining apple and chives, and serve with Melba toast.

Chapter 2

# LIGHT MEALS
# & SNACKS

*Pizza Casalinga (page 20)*

# PIZZA CASALINGA

**SERVES 6**
*Preparation time: 1 hour 45 minutes*
*Cooking time: 25 minutes*

| |
|---|
| one 283 g (10 oz) packet white bread and pizza base mix |
| 25 g (1 oz) Clover |
| 2 cloves garlic, skinned and crushed |
| 225 g (8 oz) mushrooms, wiped and sliced |
| 400 g (14 oz) can tomatoes |
| salt and pepper |
| 400 g (14 oz) Mozzarella cheese, thinly sliced |
| 100 g (4 oz) cooked ham, cut into strips |
| 50 g (2 oz) can anchovy fillets, drained |
| 10 black olives, halved and stoned |
| 20 ml (4 tsp) chopped fresh oregano or 10 ml (2 tsp) dried |
| 30 ml (2 tbsp) olive oil |

**1** Make the pizza dough according to the instructions on the packet and leave to rise.

**2** Heat the Clover in a heavy-based frying pan. Add the garlic and mushrooms and fry for about 5 minutes or until the oil is completely absorbed.

**3** Turn the risen dough out on to a floured surface and roll out to a rectangle, approximately 30 × 25 cm (12 × 10 inches). Make the edges slightly thicker than the centre. Put the dough on an oiled baking sheet.

**4** Mash the tomatoes with half of their juice so that there are no large lumps, then spread them evenly over the dough, right to the edges. Season to taste.

**5** Arrange the slices of Mozzarella over the tomatoes, then sprinkle over the strips of ham. Top with the mushrooms and anchovies, then dot with the olives.

**6** Mix together the oregano and olive oil, and add salt and pepper to taste. Drizzle over the top of the pizza.

**7** Leave the pizza to prove in a warm place for about 30 minutes, then bake in the oven at 220°C (425°F) mark 7 for 25 minutes or until the topping is melted and the dough well risen. Cut into serving portions.

# STUFFED AUBERGINES

**SERVES 4**
*Preparation time: 45 minutes*
*Cooking time: 25 minutes*

| |
|---|
| 4 small aubergines, washed and dried |
| salt and pepper |
| 30 ml (2 tbsp) olive oil |
| 25 g (1 oz) butter or Clover |
| 1 small onion, skinned and very finely chopped |
| 4 small ripe tomatoes, skinned and roughly chopped |
| 10 ml (2 tsp) chopped fresh basil or 5 ml (1 tsp) dried |
| 2 hard-boiled eggs, shelled and roughly chopped |
| 15 ml (1 tbsp) capers |
| 225 g (8 oz) Mozzarella cheese, sliced |

**1** Cut each aubergine in half lengthways and scoop out the flesh. Reserve the shells.

**2** Chop the flesh finely, then spread out on a plate and sprinkle with salt. Leave for 20 minutes to remove bitter flavour. Turn aubergine flesh into a colander. Rinse, drain and dry.

**3** Heat half the oil in a pan with the butter or Clover, add the onion and fry gently for 5 minutes until soft but not coloured. Add the aubergine flesh, tomatoes, basil and seasoning to taste.

**4** Meanwhile, put the aubergine shells in a single layer in an oiled ovenproof dish. Brush the insides with the remaining oil, then bake in the oven at 180°C (350°F) mark 4 for 10 minutes.

**5** Spoon half the tomato mixture into the bases of the aubergine shells. Cover each with a layer of chopped eggs and capers, then with a layer of cheese. Spoon the remaining tomato mixture over the tops. Return to the oven and bake for a further 15 minutes until sizzling hot. Serve immediately.

# MACARONI PIE

**SERVES 6**
*Preparation time: 35 minutes*
*Cooking time: 35 minutes*

| |
| --- |
| 115 g (4½ oz) butter or Clover |
| 30 ml (2 tbsp) olive oil |
| 1 small onion, skinned and finely chopped |
| 2 cloves garlic, skinned and crushed |
| 400 g (14 oz) can tomatoes |
| 5 ml (1 tsp) chopped fresh basil or 2.5 ml (½ tsp) dried, or mixed herbs |
| salt and pepper |
| 225 g (8 oz) large macaroni |
| 75 g (3 oz) plain flour |
| 568 ml (1 pint) milk |
| 75 g (3 oz) Gruyère cheese, grated |
| 1.25 ml (¼ tsp) freshly grated nutmeg |
| 60 ml (4 tbsp) freshly grated Parmesan cheese |
| 45 ml (3 tbsp) dried breadcrumbs |

**1** Make the tomato sauce. Melt 50 g (2 oz) of the butter or Clover in a heavy-based saucepan with the olive oil. Add the onion and garlic and fry gently for 5 minutes until soft but not coloured.

**2** Add the tomatoes and their juices with the basil and seasoning to taste, then stir with a wooden spoon to break up the tomatoes. Bring to the boil, then lower the heat and simmer for 10 minutes; stir occasionally.

**3** Meanwhile, plunge the macaroni into a large pan of boiling salted water, bring back to the boil and cook for 10 minutes or until just tender.

**4** Make the cheese sauce. Melt the remaining butter or Clover in a separate saucepan, add the flour and cook over low heat, stirring with a wooden spoon, for about 2 minutes. Remove the pan from the heat and gradually blend in the milk, stirring after each addition to prevent lumps forming. Bring to the boil slowly, stirring all the time, until the sauce thickens. Add the Gruyère cheese and seasoning to taste and stir until melted.

**5** Drain the macaroni and mix with the tomato sauce. Arrange half this mixture in a large buttered oven-proof dish.

**6** Pour over half of the cheese sauce. Repeat the layers, then sprinkle evenly with the Parmesan and breadcrumbs.

**7** Bake the pie in the oven at 190°C (375°F) mark 5 for 15 minutes, then brown under a preheated hot grill for 5 minutes. Serve hot.

# SMOKED HADDOCK SCRAMBLE

**SERVES 2**
*Preparation time: 15 minutes*
*Cooking time: 10 minutes*

| |
| --- |
| 3 eggs |
| 30 ml (2 tbsp) milk |
| 30 ml (2 tbsp) double or single cream |
| 5 ml (1 tsp) lemon juice |
| salt and pepper |
| vegetable oil, for shallow frying |
| 2 large slices white bread, crusts removed |
| 50 g (2 oz) butter or Clover |
| 100 g (4 oz) smoked haddock fillet, flaked |
| chopped fresh parsley, to garnish |

**1** In a bowl, whisk together the eggs, milk, cream, lemon juice and salt and pepper to taste. Set aside.

**2** Heat the oil in a frying pan, add the bread and fry until golden brown on both sides. Remove and drain on absorbent kitchen paper.

**3** Melt the butter or Clover in a saucepan and add the egg mixture with the fish. Cook slowly, stirring gently and continuously, until the egg mixture becomes very creamy in texture. Taste and adjust seasoning, then remove from the heat to prevent overcooking.

**4** Place the bread on a serving plate, spoon over the haddock scramble and garnish. Serve immediately.

*Left: Spicy Scotch Eggs (page 25)*
*Right: Pissaladière (page 25)*

## FETTUCCINE IN CREAMY HAM AND MUSHROOM SAUCE

**SERVES 2**
*Preparation time: 15 minutes*
*Cooking time: 15 minutes*

| |
|---|
| 225 g (8 oz) fresh or dried fettuccine or tagliatelle |
| salt and pepper |
| 50 g (2 oz) butter or Clover |
| 100 g (4 oz) button mushrooms, finely sliced |
| 2 slices smoked ham, cut into fine strips |
| freshly grated nutmeg |
| 150 ml (5 fl oz) double cream |
| 25 g (1 oz) freshly grated Parmesan cheese |

**1** Put the pasta in a large pan of boiling salted water. Cook dried pasta 8–12 minutes; fresh 2–3 minutes.

**2** Meanwhile, melt the butter or Clover in a small saucepan, add mushrooms and fry for 2–3 minutes. Add the ham and nutmeg, salt and pepper to taste. Stir in the cream and simmer for 2 minutes.

**3** Drain the pasta. Stir in the sauce and Parmesan cheese.

## SUMMER PASTA

**SERVES 2**
*Preparation time: 15 minutes*
*Cooking time: 15 minutes*

| |
|---|
| 225 g (8 oz) fresh tagliatelle, green and white mixed |
| salt and pepper |
| 2 good-sized tomatoes, skinned, deseeded and roughly chopped |
| few anchovy fillets, snipped into small pieces (optional) |
| 90 ml (6 tbsp) single cream |
| 100 g (4 oz) cooked peeled prawns |
| 113 g (4 oz) can mussels in brine |
| 5 ml (1 tsp) tomato purée |
| 1 clove garlic, skinned and crushed |
| 1 large knob of butter or Clover |
| piece of Parmesan cheese |
| 45 ml (3 tbsp) chopped fresh parsley |
| whole prawns in shells, to garnish |

**1** Cook the pasta in plenty of boiling salted water until tender.

**2** Meanwhile, place the tomatoes and anchovies, if used, in a saucepan with the cream, prawns, drained mussels, tomato purée, garlic and seasoning. Heat gently.

**3** To serve, drain the pasta and toss in the butter or Clover. Stir in the sauce. Top with shavings of Parmesan and parsley. Garnish with whole prawns in shells.

## CHICKEN LIVER AND MUSHROOM SALAD

**SERVES 2**
*Preparation time: 15 minutes*
*Cooking time: 10 minutes*

| |
|---|
| a selection of salad leaves such as radicchio, watercress, frisée, oakleaf or lamb's lettuce |
| 40 g (1½ oz) Clover |
| 225 g (8 oz) chicken livers, halved |
| 225 g (8 oz) mixed mushrooms, such as button, flat, oyster |
| 60 ml (4 tbsp) chopped fresh parsley |
| 2 spring onions, chopped |
| 30 ml (2 tbsp) sherry vinegar |
| 30 ml (2 tbsp) hazelnut oil |
| salt and pepper |
| crusty bread, to accompany |

**1** Wash the salad leaves; dry and put them in polythene bags in the refrigerator until required. Arrange on 2 plates.

**2** Melt the Clover in a large sauté pan and fry the chicken livers for 2–3 minutes until well browned. Add the mushrooms and fry for a further 5 minutes.

**3** Stir in the parsley, chopped onion, vinegar, oil and seasoning.

**4** Divide the mixture between the salad leaves and serve immediately, with crusty bread.

# PISSALADIÈRE

SERVES 6
*Preparation time: 30 minutes plus 15 minutes chilling*
*Cooking time: 1 hour*

| |
|---|
| *50 g (2 oz) butter or Clover* |
| *100 g (4 oz) plain flour* |
| *salt and pepper* |
| *30 ml (2 tbsp) water* |
| *450 g (1 lb) onions, skinned and finely sliced* |
| *2 cloves garlic, skinned and crushed* |
| *90 ml (6 tbsp) vegetable oil* |
| *225 g (8 oz) tomatoes, skinned* |
| *30 ml (2 tbsp) tomato purée* |
| *5 ml (1 tsp) fresh herbs (e.g. marjoram, thyme or sage)* |
| *anchovy fillets and black olives* |

1 Make the pastry. Cut the butter or Clover into pieces and add these to the plain flour with a pinch of salt.

2 Mix until the mixture resembles fine breadcrumbs. Add water and mix until it forms a smooth dough. Wrap and chill in a refrigerator for 15 minutes.

3 When the dough is cool, roll out the pastry and use to line a 20.5 cm (8 inch) plain flan ring. Bake blind in the oven at 200°C (400°F) mark 6 for 20 minutes.

4 Meanwhile, make the filling. Fry onions and garlic in the oil in a large saucepan for 10 minutes until very soft but not brown.

5 Slice the tomatoes, add to the pan and continue cooking for 10 minutes until the liquid has evaporated. Stir in the tomato purée, herbs and seasoning.

6 Turn the mixture into the flan case. Brush with a little oil and cook in the oven at 200°C (400°F) mark 6 for 20 minutes.

7 To serve, garnish the pissaladière with a lattice of anchovy fillets and the black olives. Serve either hot or cold.

# SPICY SCOTCH EGGS

SERVES 4
*Preparation time: 30 minutes plus 30 minutes chilling*
*Cooking time: 10 minutes*

| |
|---|
| *25 g (1 oz) Clover* |
| *1 onion, skinned and very finely chopped* |
| *10 ml (2 tsp) medium-hot curry powder* |
| *450 g (1 lb) pork sausagemeat* |
| *100 g (4 oz) mature Cheddar cheese, finely grated* |
| *salt and pepper* |
| *4 hard-boiled eggs, shelled* |
| *plain flour, for coating* |
| *1 egg, beaten* |
| *100–175 g (4–6 oz) dried breadcrumbs* |
| *vegetable oil, for deep frying* |

1 Heat the Clover in a small pan, add the onion and curry powder and fry gently for 5 minutes until soft.

2 Put the sausagemeat and cheese in a bowl, add the onion and salt and pepper to taste. Mix with your hands to combine the ingredients well together.

3 Divide the mixture into four equal portions and flatten out on a floured board or work surface.

4 Place an egg in the centre of each piece. With floured hands, shape and mould the sausagemeat around the eggs. Coat lightly with more flour.

5 Brush each Scotch egg with beaten egg, then roll in the breadcrumbs until evenly coated. Chill for 30 minutes.

6 Heat the oil in a deep-fat fryer to 170°C (325°F). Carefully lower the Scotch eggs into the oil with a slotted spoon and deep-fry for 10 minutes, turning them occasionally until golden brown on all sides. Drain and cool on absorbent kitchen paper.

*Pepper and Tomato Omelette (page 28)*

*Red Flannel Hash (page 28)*

# PEPPER AND TOMATO OMELETTE

**SERVES 2**
*Preparation time: 15 minutes*
*Cooking time: 15 minutes*

| |
|---|
| 25 g (1 oz) Clover |
| 1 medium onion, skinned and sliced |
| 2 cloves garlic, skinned and crushed |
| 1 green pepper, cored, seeded and sliced |
| 1 red pepper, cored, seeded and sliced |
| 4 tomatoes, skinned and sliced |
| 5 eggs |
| pinch of dried mixed herbs, or to taste |
| salt and pepper |
| 50 g (2 oz) hard mature cheese (e.g. Parmesan, Farmhouse Cheddar), grated |

**1** Heat the Clover in a non-stick frying pan. Add the onion and garlic and fry gently for 5 minutes until soft.

**2** Add the pepper slices and the tomatoes and fry for a further 2–3 minutes, stirring frequently.

**3** In a jug, beat the eggs lightly with the herbs and seasoning to taste. Pour into the pan, allowing the egg to run to the sides.

**4** Draw in the vegetable mixture with a palette knife so that the mixture runs on to the base of the pan. Cook over moderate heat for 5 minutes until the underside of the omelette is set.

**5** Sprinkle the top of the omelette with the grated cheese, then put under a preheated hot grill for 2–3 minutes until set and browned. Slide on to a serving plate and cut into wedges to serve.

# RED FLANNEL HASH

**SERVES 4**
*Preparation time: 20 minutes*
*Cooking time: 35 minutes*

| |
|---|
| 450 g (1 lb) potatoes, scrubbed |
| salt and pepper |
| 225 g (8 oz) salt beef or corned beef, chopped |
| 1 medium onion, skinned and finely chopped |
| 5 ml (1 tsp) garlic salt |
| 225 g (8 oz) cooked beetroot, diced |
| 30 ml (2 tbsp) chopped fresh parsley |
| 50 g (2 oz) Clover |

**1** Cook the potatoes in their skins in lightly salted boiling water for about 20 minutes or until tender when pierced with a fork.

**2** Drain the potatoes, leave until cool enough to handle, then peel off the skins with your fingers. Dice the flesh.

**3** Put the diced potatoes into a large bowl, add the beef, onion, garlic salt, beetroot and parsley and toss to combine. Add pepper to taste.

**4** Heat the Clover in a heavy-based skillet or frying pan until very hot. Add the hash mixture and spread evenly with a fish slice or spatula.

**5** Lower the heat to moderate and cook the hash, uncovered, for 10–15 minutes. Break up and turn frequently with the slice or spatula, so that the hash becomes evenly browned. Serve hot.

# Chapter 3

# MEAT

# LAMB AND ROSEMARY PILAFF

**SERVES 4**
*Preparation time: 20 minutes*
*Cooking time: 50 minutes*

| |
|---|
| *450 g (1 lb) lean boneless lamb* |
| *40 g (1½ oz) Clover* |
| *15 ml (1 tbsp) dried rosemary* |
| *2 medium onions, skinned and sliced* |
| *225 g (8 oz) long-grain brown rice* |
| *750 ml (1¼ pints) stock* |
| *salt and pepper* |
| *225 g (8 oz) courgettes, trimmed and cut into fat sticks* |
| *75 g (3 oz) no-soak dried apricots, sliced* |

**1** Cut the meat into small cubes. Heat the Clover in a medium-sized flameproof casserole. Add the meat and rosemary and fry together over a high heat until the meat is beginning to brown. Remove from the pan.

**2** Add the onion slices and lightly brown. Rinse and drain the rice then stir into the pan with the stock and seasoning.

**3** Replace the meat, cover the pan and simmer for about 25 minutes. Stir the courgettes and apricots into the casserole, which is now ready to cook gently.

**4** Cover again and simmer for a further 15–20 minutes, or until most of the liquid is absorbed and the meat is quite tender. Adjust seasoning.

# MINTED LAMB GRILL

**SERVES 4**
*Preparation time: 15 minutes plus 1 hour marinating*
*Cooking time: 15 minutes*

| |
|---|
| *4 lamb chump chops* |
| *30 ml (2 tbsp) chopped fresh mint or 15 ml (1 tbsp) dried* |
| *20 ml (4 tsp) white wine vinegar* |
| *30 ml (2 tbsp) clear honey* |
| *salt and pepper* |
| *fresh mint sprigs, to garnish* |

**1** Trim any excess fat off the chump chops using a pair of sharp kitchen scissors.

**2** With a knife, slash both sides of the chops to a depth of about 5 mm (¼ inch).

**3** Make the marinade. Mix the mint, vinegar, honey and seasonings together, stirring well.

**4** Place a sheet of foil in the grill pan and turn up the edges to prevent the marinade running into the pan.

**5** Place the chops side by side on the foil and spoon over the marinade. Leave in a cool place for about 1 hour, basting occasionally.

**6** Grill under a moderate heat for 5–6 minutes on each side, turning once only. Baste with the marinade during the cooking time. Garnish with mint before serving.

*Right:  Minted Lamb Grill*

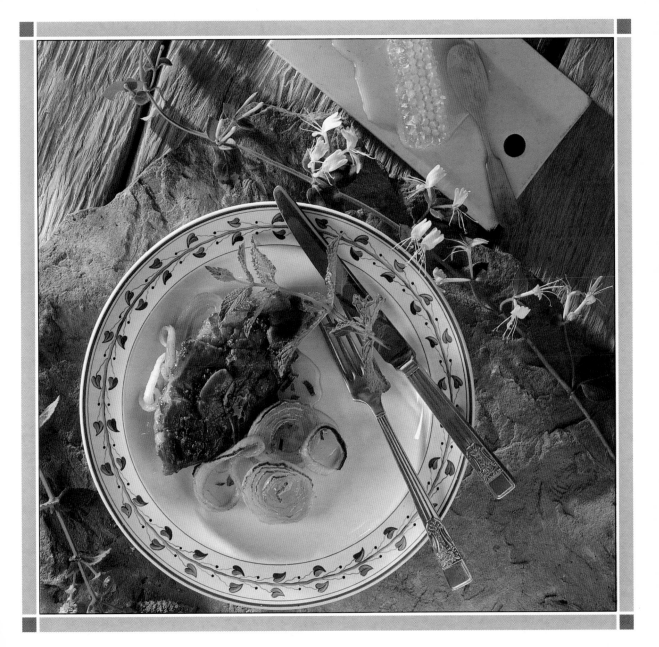

# HONEYED LAMB NOISETTES

## SERVES 6
*Preparation time: 15 minutes plus marinating overnight*
*Cooking time: 20 minutes*

| |
|---|
| 2 large lemons |
| 12 lean lamb noisettes, about 75–100 g (3–4 oz) each |
| 30 ml (2 tbsp) chopped fresh thyme or 5 ml (1 tsp) dried |
| 30 ml (2 tbsp) fresh chopped rosemary or 10 ml (2 tsp) dried |
| bay leaves |
| 2 cloves garlic, skinned and crushed |
| 1 cm ($\frac{1}{2}$ inch) piece fresh root ginger, peeled and grated (optional) |
| 120 ml (8 tbsp) clear honey |
| 60 ml (4 tbsp) vegetable oil |
| salt and pepper |
| fresh thyme and rosemary sprigs, to garnish |

1 Pare the rind off 1 lemon. Cut into fine strips. Cover and set aside.

2 Place the lamb in a shallow, non-metallic dish. Sprinkle over the herbs, adding 1 bay leaf.

3 Whisk together the grated rind of the remaining whole lemon, 90 ml (6 tbsp) lemon juice, the crushed garlic, ginger (if wished), the honey, oil and seasoning. Pour over the lamb. Cover and leave to marinate in the refrigerator overnight.

4 Drain the marinade from the lamb and strain into a small saucepan. Place the meat on a rack over the grill pan. Cook under a hot grill for about 7 minutes on each side. Transfer to an ovenproof serving dish with a slotted spoon. Cover lightly with foil and keep warm in a low oven.

5 Carefully pour the grill pan juices into the strained marinade. Stir in the strips of lemon rind. Bring to the boil and simmer, stirring occasionally, for about 2–3 minutes, or until syrupy. Adjust seasoning. Spoon over the noisettes. Garnish with bay leaves and sprigs of fresh thyme and rosemary to serve.

# PORK FILLET WITH WHITE WINE AND MUSHROOMS

## SERVES 6
*Preparation time: 20 minutes*
*Cooking time: 40 minutes*

| |
|---|
| 1 kg (2$\frac{1}{4}$ lb) pork fillet (tenderloin) |
| vegetable oil, for frying |
| 65 g (2$\frac{1}{2}$ oz) butter or Clover |
| 2 medium onions, skinned and chopped |
| 225 g (8 oz) button mushrooms |
| 45 ml (3 tbsp) plain flour |
| 150 ml ($\frac{1}{4}$ pint) beef stock |
| 150 ml ($\frac{1}{4}$ pint) dry white wine |
| salt and pepper |
| twelve 1 cm ($\frac{1}{2}$ inch) slices of French bread |
| chopped fresh parsley, to garnish |

1 Cut the pork fillet into slices and flatten slightly with a rolling pin. Heat 30 ml (2 tbsp) of the oil in a frying pan, add the pork and brown quickly. Remove from the pan and set aside.

2 Melt 50 g (2 oz) of the butter or Clover in the frying pan, add the onion and fry for 5 minutes.

3 Add the mushrooms to the pan, increase the heat and fry for 1–2 minutes, tossing constantly.

4 Blend the flour into the juices in the pan, with the remaining butter or Clover. Cook, stirring, for 1–2 minutes, then gradually blend in the stock, wine and salt and pepper. Simmer for 2–3 minutes.

5 Return the meat to the pan, cover and cook for 20–25 minutes, or until the pork is fork tender.

6 Meanwhile, heat some oil in a frying pan, add the French bread slices and fry until golden brown on each side. Drain well on absorbent kitchen paper.

7 Serve the pork hot, sprinkled liberally with chopped parsley and garnished with French bread.

# PORK STEAKS WITH PEPPERS

**SERVES 4**
*Preparation time: 10 minutes*
*Cooking time: 10 minutes*

| |
|---|
| 40 g (1½ oz) Clover |
| 1 medium onion, skinned and chopped |
| 2.5 cm (1 inch) piece fresh root ginger, peeled and finely grated |
| 1 clove garlic, skinned and crushed |
| 4 boneless pork loin steaks, each weighing 150 g (5 oz) |
| 1 red pepper, seeded and thinly sliced |
| 1 green pepper, seeded and thinly sliced |
| 45 ml (3 tbsp) dry sherry |
| 30 ml (2 tbsp) soy sauce |
| 150 ml (¼ pint) unsweetened pineapple juice |
| salt and pepper |

1  Heat the Clover in a large frying pan, add the onion, ginger and garlic and gently fry for 5 minutes, until soft. Push to one side of the pan.

2  Add the steaks and brown on both sides, then add the remaining ingredients and mix thoroughly together.

3  Cover tightly and simmer gently for 8–10 minutes, until the steaks are tender and the peppers are soft. Transfer the steaks and peppers to warmed serving plates. Bring the remaining liquid in the pan to the boil and boil for 2–3 minutes until reduced slightly. Spoon over the steaks and serve with boiled rice.

# PORK AND VEGETABLE STIR FRY

**SERVES 4**
*Preparation time: 20 minutes*
*Cooking time: 10 minutes*

| |
|---|
| 5 ml (1 tsp) cornflour |
| 30 ml (2 tbsp) vinegar |
| 30 ml (2 tbsp) soy sauce |
| 15 ml (1 tbsp) honey |
| salt and pepper |
| 50 g (2 oz) Clover |
| 450 g (1 lb) pork fillet (tenderloin), cut into strips |
| 175 g (6 oz) carrots, peeled and cut into fine strips |
| 25 g (1 oz) piece fresh root ginger, peeled and finely chopped |
| 1 bunch spring onions, each one cut into 3 or 4 pieces |
| 1 green or yellow pepper, shredded |
| 175 g (6 oz) fresh beansprouts, rinsed |

1  Mix the cornflour to a smooth paste with 60 ml (4 tbsp) water. Stir in the vinegar, soy sauce, honey and seasoning.

2  Heat the Clover in a wok or large frying pan. Add the pork, carrot and ginger and stir-fry over a high heat for 2–3 minutes or until browned.

3  Add the onions, pepper and beansprouts and continue cooking over a high heat for 2 minutes. Stir in the cornflour mixture, and cook until it thickens. Serve with boiled rice or fine noodles.

*Left:  Honeyed Lamb Noisettes (page 32)*
*Centre:  Lamb and Rosemary Pilaff (page 30)*
*Right:  Pork Fillet with White Wine and Mushrooms*
*(page 32)*

# Gingered Beef Casserole

**SERVES 4**
*Preparation time: 20 minutes*
*Cooking time: 3 hours 20 minutes*

| |
|---|
| 50 g (2 oz) Clover |
| 900 g (2 lb) chuck steak, trimmed of fat and cut into 5 cm (2 inch) cubes |
| 7.5 cm (3 inch) piece fresh root ginger, peeled and cut into thin slivers |
| 1 medium onion, skinned and thinly sliced |
| 1 garlic clove, skinned and crushed |
| 30–45 ml (2–3 tbsp) honey, according to taste |
| 30 ml (2 tbsp) tomato purée |
| 15 ml (1 tbsp) wine vinegar |
| 600 ml (1 pint) beef stock |
| salt and pepper |

**1** Heat the Clover in a flameproof casserole, add the cubes of beef and fry over moderate heat until browned on all sides. Remove with a slotted spoon and set aside.

**2** Lower the heat, add the ginger, onion and garlic and fry gently, stirring constantly, for about 10 minutes until softened.

**3** Add the honey, tomato purée and wine vinegar and stir well into the ginger mixture. Pour in the stock and bring to the boil.

**4** Return the beef to the casserole and add salt and pepper to taste. Cover and cook in the oven at 150°C (300°F) mark 2 for 2½–3 hours, until the beef is very tender. Taste and adjust seasoning before serving.

# Stilton Steaks

**SERVES 4**
*Preparation time: 10 minutes*
*Cooking time: 10 minutes*

| |
|---|
| 175 g (6 oz) Blue Stilton cheese |
| 25 g (1 oz) butter or Clover, softened |
| 50–75 g (2–3 oz) shelled walnuts, finely chopped |
| salt and pepper |
| 4 sirloin or fillet steaks, about 125–175 g (4–6 oz) each |
| 45 ml (3 tbsp) olive or vegetable oil |
| 10 ml (2 tsp) chopped fresh sage or 5 ml (1 tsp) dried |

**1** Put the cheese in a bowl and mash with a fork. Add the butter or Clover and walnuts and mix in with salt and pepper to taste. (Add salt sparingly as Stilton cheese tends to be quite salty.)

**2** Trim any fat off the steaks, then place on the grill rack. Brush with half the oil, then sprinkle with half the sage and plenty of pepper.

**3** Put under a preheated hot grill and cook for 2–4 minutes on each side, according to the thickness of the steaks and how well done you like them. When you turn the steaks over to cook the other side, brush with the remaining oil and sprinkle with the remaining sage and pepper.

**4** Remove the steaks from under the grill, sprinkle the cheese and nut mixture evenly over them and press down with a palette knife. Grill for a further minute or until the topping is melted and bubbling. Serve hot.

# ESCALOPES WITH HERBS

**SERVES 4**
*Preparation time: 10 minutes*
*Cooking time: 20 minutes*

| |
|---|
| 4 pork or veal escalopes, about 100 g (4 oz) each |
| 45 ml (3 tbsp) plain flour |
| salt and pepper |
| 25 g (1 oz) butter or Clover |
| 100 ml (4 fl oz) dry white wine |
| 30 ml (2 tbsp) chopped fresh herbs, e.g., parsley, chervil, tarragon and chives |
| 60 ml (4 tbsp) double cream |
| lemon wedges, to serve |

**1** Using a rolling pin, flatten each escalope between 2 sheets of dampened greaseproof paper or cling film.

**2** Mix the flour with a little salt and pepper and use to coat the escalopes.

**3** Melt the butter or Clover in a large frying pan, add the escalopes and fry briskly for 1–2 minutes on each side until browned. (You may have to fry in two batches, depending on the size of the pan.) Lower the heat and continue to cook for a further 4 minutes on each side until tender. Transfer the meat to a serving dish, cover and keep hot in a low oven.

**4** Add the white wine to the pan and bring slowly to the boil, stirring to scrape up any sediment left in the pan. Stir in the herbs and cream with salt and pepper to taste. Simmer very gently for about 5 minutes, until slightly thickened.

**5** Pour the sauce over the escalopes and serve immediately, with lemon wedges.

# PAN-FRIED VEAL WITH MUSTARD AND CREAM

**SERVES 4**
*Preparation time: 10 minutes*
*Cooking time: 15 minutes*

| |
|---|
| 4 veal escalopes, about 100–175 g (4–6 oz) each |
| 40 g (1½ oz) butter or Clover |
| 150 ml (¼ pint) veal or chicken stock |
| 150 ml (¼ pint) single cream |
| 15 ml (1 tbsp) wholegrain mustard |
| juice of ½ lemon |
| salt and pepper |
| chopped fresh parsley, to garnish |

**1** Cut the veal into thin, pencil-like strips about 6.5 cm (2½ inches) long. Melt the butter or Clover in a frying pan and, when foaming, add the veal. Fry over high heat for 2–3 minutes, stirring constantly until lightly browned.

**2** Lift the veal out of the pan with a slotted spoon and transfer to a plate.

**3** Add the stock to the pan and boil, until reduced by half, stirring constantly.

**4** Stir in the cream, mustard, the lemon juice and browned veal. Season to taste with salt and pepper and simmer for 5 minutes. Serve immediately, garnished with plenty of chopped parsley.

*Pork Steaks with Peppers (page 33)*

*Liver and Bacon with Potato Pancakes (page 41)*

# ALMOND BEEF WITH CELERY

**SERVES 6**
*Preparation time: 30 minutes*
*Cooking time: 1½ hours*

| |
|---|
| 900 g (2 lb) shin of beef |
| 45 ml (3 tbsp) vegetable oil |
| 15 ml (1 tbsp) plain flour |
| 90 ml (6 tbsp) ground almonds |
| 1 garlic clove, skinned and crushed |
| 300 ml (½ pint) beef stock |
| salt and pepper |
| 4 celery sticks |
| 25 g (1 oz) butter or Clover |
| 50 g (2 oz) flaked almonds |

**1** Cut the beef into 2.5 cm (1 inch) pieces. Heat the oil in a flameproof casserole, add the meat a few pieces at a time and brown well, removing each batch with a slotted spoon.

**2** Return all the meat to the pan. Stir in the flour, ground almonds and crushed garlic. Stir over the heat for 1 minute, then pour in the beef stock. Bring to the boil and season to taste with salt and pepper.

**3** Cover the casserole and cook in the oven at 180°C (350°F) mark 4 for about 1½ hours or until the meat is tender.

**4** Ten minutes before the end of cooking time, slice the celery. Melt the butter or Clover in a large frying pan, add the celery and flaked almonds and sauté for about 6 minutes or until golden brown.

**5** Taste and adjust the seasoning of the beef. Sprinkle with the celery and almond mixture and serve at once.

# PORK ESCALOPES WITH SAGE

**SERVES 4**
*Preparation time: 15 minutes*
*Cooking time: 6 minutes*

| |
|---|
| 450 g (1 lb) pork fillet |
| 1 egg, beaten |
| 100 g (4 oz) fresh brown breadcrumbs |
| 30 ml (2 tbsp) fresh sage or 10 ml (2 tsp) dried |
| grated rind of 1 lemon |
| 75 g (3 oz) butter or Clover, melted |
| lemon wedges, to serve |

**1** Using a sharp knife, trim any excess fat from the pork fillet and cut the meat into 5 mm (¼ inch) slices.

**2** Beat out into even thinner slices between two sheets of greaseproof paper, using a meat cleaver or a wooden rolling pin.

**3** Coat the escalopes with the beaten egg. Then mix together the breadcrumbs, sage and grated lemon rind and coat the pork escalopes.

**4** Lay in the base of a grill pan lined with foil (this quantity will need to be grilled in two batches). Brush with melted butter or Clover. Grill for about 3 minutes each side. Serve with lemon wedges.

# LIVER AND BACON WITH POTATO PANCAKES

**SERVES 4**
*Preparation time: 35 minutes*
*Cooking time: 35 minutes*

| |
|---|
| 2 large potatoes, peeled |
| 1 egg, beaten |
| 60 ml (4 tbsp) self-raising flour |
| salt and pepper |
| vegetable oil and Clover, for frying |
| 450 g (1 lb) lamb's liver, cut thickly |
| 25 g (1 oz) plain flour |
| 8 rashers of back bacon |
| 2 medium onions, skinned and finely sliced |
| 10 ml (2 tsp) wine vinegar |
| 30 ml (2 tbsp) chopped fresh parsley, to garnish |

**1** Grate the potatoes finely. Place in a sieve and rinse under cold water. Leave to drain for about 15 minutes. Wrap the potato in a clean tea towel and squeeze out any excess moisture.

**2** Put the grated potatoes in a bowl. Add the egg, self-raising flour and salt and pepper to taste, then mix well together.

**3** Heat enough oil in a frying pan to come 0.5 cm ($\frac{1}{4}$ inch) up the sides. When hot, add large spoonfuls of potato mixture, pressing them into flat pancakes with a spatula or fish slice.

**4** Cook the pancakes for about 5 minutes on each side until golden brown. Remove from the pan and drain on absorbent kitchen paper. Keep hot in the oven while cooking the liver.

**5** Remove any ducts from the liver and discard. Dip the liver in the plain flour seasoned with salt and pepper. Heat a knob of Clover in a frying pan, add the liver and fry for 3–4 minutes on each side (it should still be slightly pink inside). Cover and keep hot.

**6** Add the bacon to the pan and fry over brisk heat until crisp. Keep hot, but do not cover as it will become soggy.

**7** Add the onions to the pan and cook for 5 minutes until just beginning to brown. Remove from the pan and arrange on a serving dish. Top with the liver and bacon and keep warm.

**8** Add the vinegar and 45 ml (3 tbsp) water to the frying pan. Bring to the boil, scraping up any sediment from the bottom of the pan. Pour over the liver and bacon, then garnish with chopped parsley. Serve with the pancakes.

# Chapter 4

# CHICKEN & POULTRY

*Spanish Chicken and Rice (page 48)*

# CHICKEN PAPRIKASH

**SERVES 4**
*Preparation time: 20 minutes*
*Cooking time: 1 hour 15 minutes*

4 chicken quarters, cut in half
50 g (2 oz) flour
salt and pepper
50 g (2 oz) butter or Clover
450 g (1 lb) onions, skinned and sliced
1 red pepper, cored, seeded and sliced
15 ml (1 tbsp) mild paprika
cayenne pepper, to taste
1 clove garlic, skinned and crushed
400 g (14 oz) can tomatoes
300 ml ($\frac{1}{2}$ pint) chicken stock
1 bay leaf
150 ml (5 fl oz) soured cream

**1** Toss the chicken pieces in the flour, liberally seasoned with salt and pepper, to coat.

**2** Melt the butter or Clover in a frying pan and fry the chicken joints until golden brown. Transfer the joints to a casserole large enough to take them in a single layer.

**3** Add the onions and red pepper to the frying pan and fry gently for 5 minutes until soft. Stir in the paprika, cayenne pepper, garlic and any remaining flour. Cook gently, stirring, for a few minutes.

**4** Add the tomatoes with their juice, the stock and bay leaf. Season and bring to the boil. Pour over the chicken.

**5** Cover tightly and cook in the oven at 170°C (325°F) mark 3 for about 1 hour until the chicken is tender. Discard the bay leaf.

**6** Stir half the soured cream into the casserole. Spoon the remaining soured cream over the top and serve immediately.

# PARSLEY CHICKEN WITH CASHEWS

**SERVES 8**
*Preparation time: 15 minutes*
*Cooking time: 35 minutes*

50 g (2 oz) creamed coconut
bunch chopped fresh parsley
1 large onion, skinned and sliced
8 chicken breast fillets, about 100 g (4 oz) each
60 ml (4 tbsp) flour
30 ml (2 tbsp) ground coriander
30 ml (2 tbsp) ground cumin
10 ml (2 tsp) ground turmeric
salt and pepper
vegetable oil
25 g (1 oz) butter or Clover
150 g (5 oz) salted cashew nuts
600 ml (1 pint) chicken stock
60 ml (4 tbsp) lemon juice

**1** Break up the coconut and dissolve in 150 ml ($\frac{1}{4}$ pint) boiling water. Chop enough parsley to give about 90 ml (6 tbsp).

**2** Split each chicken breast to give two thinner fillets. Mix together the flour, spices and seasoning. Use to coat the chicken.

**3** Heat 60 ml (4 tbsp) oil and the butter or Clover in a large flameproof casserole or sauté pan. Brown the chicken pieces half at a time; remove from pan. Add the onion and 100 g (4 oz) nuts, with a little more oil if necessary, and lightly brown, stirring frequently.

**4** Mix in any remaining flour followed by the coconut, water, the stock, 75 ml (5 tbsp) parsley and the lemon juice.

**5** Return the chicken to the pan. Bring to the boil, cover and simmer for about 20 minutes, or until the chicken is quite tender, stirring occasionally. Uncover and bubble down the juices until slightly thickened. Adjust seasoning and sprinkle with the remaining chopped parsley and nuts.

# CHICKEN WITH TARRAGON SAUCE

**SERVES 6**
*Preparation time: 10 minutes*
*Cooking time: 20 minutes*

| |
| --- |
| 6 chicken breast fillets, skinned |
| 75 g (3 oz) butter or Clover |
| 25 g (1 oz) flour |
| 400 ml (¾ pint) chicken stock |
| 30 ml (2 tbsp) tarragon vinegar |
| 10 ml (2 tsp) French mustard |
| 5 ml (1 tsp) fresh tarragon, chopped, or 2.5 ml (½ tsp) dried tarragon |
| 50 g (2 oz) Cheddar cheese, grated |
| salt and pepper |
| 150 ml (5 fl oz) single cream |

**1** In a covered pan, slowly cook the chicken breasts in 50 g (2 oz) of the butter or Clover, for about 20 minutes, until tender, turning once.

**2** Meanwhile, melt the remaining butter or Clover in a pan, stir in the flour and cook for 1 minute, stirring. Off the heat, gradually stir in the stock and vinegar.

**3** Stir in the mustard, tarragon and cheese; bring to the boil, stirring. Season, simmer for 3 minutes. Remove from heat and add the cream.

**4** Heat gently without boiling. Place drained chicken on a serving dish and spoon over the sauce.

# CHICKEN LIVER BOLOGNESE

**SERVES 4**
*Preparation time: 15 minutes*
*Cooking time: 30 minutes*

| |
| --- |
| 2 medium onions, skinned and chopped |
| 100 g (4 oz) carrots, peeled and chopped |
| 100 g (4 oz) celery, chopped |
| 50 g (2 oz) Clover |
| 100 g (4 oz) streaky bacon, rinded |
| 450 g (1 lb) chicken livers, chopped |
| 45 ml (3 tbsp) tomato purée |
| 150 ml (¼ pint) red wine |
| 150 ml (¼ pint) chicken stock |
| 2.5 ml (½ tsp) dried oregano |
| 1 bay leaf |
| salt and pepper |
| 275 g (10 oz) spaghetti |
| grated Parmesan cheese, to serve |

**1** Melt half of the Clover in a deep frying pan and fry the chopped vegetables until golden.

**2** Snip the bacon into the pan, add the chicken livers and fry for about 5 minutes until the livers are browned on the outside and pink, but set, inside.

**3** Stir in the tomato purée, red wine and stock. Add the oregano, bay leaf and seasoning, then bring to the boil. Lower heat, cover and simmer for 20 minutes.

**4** Cook the spaghetti in boiling salted water for about 11 minutes until it is tender.

**5** Drain the spaghetti and toss in the remaining Clover or in 25 g (1 oz) butter. Season with pepper. Serve with the chicken liver sauce, and grated Parmesan.

*Chicken Paprikash (page 44)*

Stoved Chicken (page 48)

# SPANISH CHICKEN AND RICE

**SERVES 4**
*Preparation time: 15 minutes*
*Cooking time: 1 hour 30 minutes*

4 chicken quarters, halved
30 ml (2 tbsp) flour
salt and pepper
45 ml (3 tbsp) vegetable oil
25 g (1 oz) Clover
1 medium onion, skinned and chopped
400 g (14 oz) can tomatoes
170 g (6 oz) can pimentoes, drained and sliced
2 chicken stock cubes, crumbled
8 stuffed olives
175 g (6 oz) long grain rice
225 g (8 oz) chorizo sausages, cut into 1 cm ($\frac{1}{2}$ inch) slices
100 g (4 oz) frozen peas
watercress sprigs, to garnish

**1** Toss the chicken pieces in the flour seasoned with salt and pepper. Heat the oil and Clover in a large saucepan, brown the chicken on all sides and remove. Add the onion and fry until golden brown.

**2** Drain the tomatoes and add enough water to make the juice up to 450 ml ($\frac{3}{4}$ pint).

**3** Return the chicken to the pan. Add the tomato juice, the tomatoes and the next five ingredients. Season to taste.

**4** Cover the pan tightly and simmer gently for 45 minutes, forking carefully through the rice occasionally to prevent it sticking.

**5** Add the peas to the pan, cover again and simmer for a further 30 minutes until the chicken is tender. Before serving, taste and adjust seasoning and garnish with the sprigs of watercress.

# STOVED CHICKEN

**SERVES 4**
*Preparation time: 30 minutes*
*Cooking time: 2 hours 10 minutes*

25 g (1 oz) butter or Clover
15 ml (1 tbsp) vegetable oil
4 chicken quarters, halved
100 g (4 oz) lean back bacon, rinded and chopped
1.1 kg ($2\frac{1}{2}$ lb) floury potatoes, such as King Edwards, peeled and cut into 0.5 cm ($\frac{1}{4}$ inch) slices
2 large onions, skinned and sliced
salt and pepper
10 ml (2 tsp) chopped fresh thyme or 2.5 ml ($\frac{1}{2}$ tsp) dried thyme
600 ml (1 pint) chicken stock
fresh chives, to garnish

**1** Heat half the butter or Clover and the oil in a large frying pan and fry the chicken and bacon for 5 minutes, until lightly browned.

**2** Place a thick layer of potato slices, then onion slices, in the base of a large ovenproof casserole. Season well, add the thyme and dot with half the remaining butter or Clover.

**3** Add the chicken and bacon, season to taste and dot with half the remaining butter or Clover. Cover with the remaining onions and finally a layer of potatoes. Season and dot with butter or Clover. Pour over the stock.

**4** Cover and bake at 150°C (300°F) mark 2 for about 2 hours, until the chicken is tender and the potatoes are cooked, adding a little more hot stock if necessary. Just before serving, sprinkle with snipped chives.

*Duckling with Green Peas (page 51)*

# TURKEY PUFF PIE

### SERVES 4–6
### *Preparation time: 50 minutes*
### *Cooking time: 40 minutes*

| |
|---|
| 700 g (1½ lb) cooked turkey or chicken meat |
| 100 g (4 oz) cooked ham, cut into bite-size pieces |
| 25 g (1 oz) butter or Clover |
| 600 ml (1 pint) chicken stock |
| 1 medium onion, skinned and chopped |
| 4 leeks, trimmed, washed and thickly sliced |
| 2 large carrots, peeled and thickly sliced |
| 45 ml (3 tbsp) plain flour |
| 150 ml (¼ pint) milk |
| 60 ml (4 tbsp) double cream |
| salt and pepper |
| 225 g (8 oz) frozen puff pastry, defrosted |
| 1 egg, beaten, to glaze |

1  Remove the turkey or chicken meat from the bones, discarding the skin. Cut into bite-size chunks.

2  Put turkey and ham in a 1.1 litre (2 pint) pie dish.

3  Melt the butter or Clover in a saucepan, add the onion, carrots and leeks and fry gently until softened. Sprinkle in the flour and cook for 1–2 minutes, stirring, then gradually add the stock. Bring to the boil and simmer, stirring, until thick, then stir in the milk and cream with salt and pepper to taste. Pour into the pie dish and leave for about 30 minutes until cold.

4  Roll out the pastry on a floured work surface until about 2.5 cm (1 inch) larger all round than the pie dish.

5  Cut off a strip from all round the edge of the pastry. Place the strip on the moistened rim of the pie dish, moisten the strip, then place the pastry lid on top.

6  Press the edge firmly to seal, then knock up and flute. Make a hole in the centre of the pie and use the pastry trimmings to decorate.

7  Brush the pastry with beaten egg, then bake in the oven at 190°C (375°F) mark 5 for 30 minutes until puffed up and golden brown. Serve hot.

# TURKEY IN SPICED YOGURT

### SERVES 6
### *Preparation time: 20 minutes plus overnight marinating*
### *Cooking time: 1 hour 30 minutes*

| |
|---|
| turkey leg on the bone, about 1.1 kg (2½ lb) in weight |
| 7.5 ml (1½ tsp) ground cumin |
| 7.5 ml (1½ tsp) ground coriander |
| 2.5 ml (½ tsp) ground turmeric |
| 2.5 ml (½ tsp) ground ginger |
| salt and pepper |
| 275 g (10 oz) natural yogurt |
| 30 ml (2 tbsp) lemon juice |
| 40 g (1½ oz) Clover |
| 225 g (8 oz) onions, skinned and sliced |
| 45 ml (3 tbsp) desiccated coconut |
| 30 ml (2 tbsp) plain flour |
| 150 ml (¼ pint) chicken stock or water |
| chopped fresh parsley, to garnish |

1  Cut the turkey meat off the bone into large fork-sized pieces, discarding the skin (there should be about 900 g [2 lb] meat).

2  Make the marinade. In a large bowl mix the spices with the seasoning, yogurt and lemon juice. Stir well until evenly blended. Fold through the turkey meat until coated with the yogurt mixture. Cover tightly with cling film and refrigerate overnight.

3  Melt the Clover in a medium flameproof casserole, add the onions and fry for about 5 minutes until lightly brown. Add the coconut and flour and fry gently, stirring, for about 1 minute.

4  Off the heat stir in the turkey with its marinade, and the stock. Return to the heat and bring slowly to the boil, stirring all the time to prevent sticking.

5  Cover tightly and cook in the oven at 170°C (325°F) mark 3 for 1–1¼ hours or until the turkey is tender when tested with a fork. To serve, adjust the seasoning and serve garnished with parsley.

# DUCKLING WITH GREEN PEAS

**SERVES 4**
*Preparation time: 15 minutes*
*Cooking time: 2 hours 40 minutes*

| |
|---|
| 1 oven-ready duckling, weighing about 2 kg (4½ lb) |
| salt and pepper |
| 16 pickling or small onions, skinned and chopped |
| 50 g (2 oz) smoked streaky bacon, rinded and diced |
| 450 g (1 lb) shelled fresh or frozen peas |
| 60 ml (4 tbsp) chicken stock |
| few sprigs of fresh herbs, such as savory, thyme, mint |

**1** Weigh the duckling, prick the skin all over with a sharp skewer or fork and rub with salt. Place duckling on a wire rack or trivet in a roasting tin. Roast in a preheated oven at 180°C (350°F) mark 4 for 30–35 minutes per 450 g (1 lb).

**2** Thirty minutes before the end of cooking time, drain off the fat from the roasting tin, transferring 30 ml (2 tbsp) of it to a saucepan, and discarding the remainder. Add the onions to the pan and cook, turning frequently, until lightly browned. Add the bacon and cook for 2 minutes, until the fat starts to run.

**3** If using fresh peas, blanch them for 3 minutes, refresh and drain well. Do not blanch frozen peas. Mix the peas with the onions, bacon and herbs and season to taste with pepper.

**4** Stir the stock into the sediment in the roasting tin, then stir in the pea mixture. Return the duckling to the roasting tin, still on the rack, and continue cooking for the remaining 30 minutes. Serve the duckling on a large platter surrounded by the vegetables and the cooking juices.

# SWEET AND SOUR DUCK

**SERVES 4**
*Preparation time: 10 minutes*
*Cooking time: 1 hour*

| |
|---|
| 4 duck portions |
| salt and pepper |
| 60 ml (4 tbsp) soy sauce |
| 45 ml (3 tbsp) soft brown sugar |
| 45 ml (3 tbsp) honey |
| 45 ml (3 tbsp) wine or cider vinegar |
| 30 ml (2 tbsp) dry sherry |
| juice of 1 orange |
| 150 ml (¼ pint) water |
| 2.5 ml (½ tsp) ground ginger |
| few orange slices and watercress sprigs, to garnish |

**1** Prick the duck portions all over with a fork, then sprinkle the skin liberally with salt and pepper.

**2** Place on a rack in a roasting tin and roast in a preheated oven at 190°C (375°F) mark 5 for 45–60 minutes, until the skin is crisp and the juices run clear when the thickest part of each joint is pierced with a skewer.

**3** Meanwhile, make the sauce. Mix together all the remaining ingredients in a saucepan and bring to the boil. Simmer, stirring constantly, for about 5 minutes to allow the flavours to blend and the sauce to thicken slightly. Add salt and pepper to taste.

**4** Trim the duck joints neatly by cutting off any knuckles or wing joints. Arrange the duck on a warmed serving platter and coat with some of the sauce. Garnish with orange and watercress. Serve remaining sauce separately.

*Turkey Puff Pie (page 50) with Gruyère Potatoes (page 70)*

*Chapter 5*

# FISH
# & SEAFOOD

# GRATIN OF SEAFOOD

**SERVES 2**
*Preparation time: 25 minutes*
*Cooking time: 50 minutes*

| |
|---|
| 550 g (1¼ lb) old potatoes |
| salt and pepper |
| 60 ml (4 tbsp) milk |
| Clover |
| 175 g (6 oz) salmon steak |
| 175 g (6 oz) cod steak |
| 2 medium-sized scallops |
| 150 ml (¼ pint) dry white wine |
| 2.5 ml (½ tsp) dried dill |
| 50 g (2 oz) cooked peeled prawns |
| 15 ml (1 tbsp) flour |
| 30 ml (2 tbsp) double cream |
| a little grated Cheddar cheese |
| dill or parsley sprigs, to garnish (optional) |

**1** Peel the potatoes, cut into chunks and cook in boiling salted water until tender; drain. Mash with the milk, a little Clover and seasoning; cool slightly.

**2** Pipe around the edges of two shallow individual gratin dishes—about 600 ml (1 pint) each.

**3** Cut the salmon and cod into 2.5 cm (1 inch) chunks, discarding skin and bones. Divide the scallops into three or four pieces, removing the black line and any membranes. Place these fish in a medium-sized saucepan. Pour over the wine with 150 ml (¼ pint) water and add the dill and seasoning. Bring slowly to the boil, cover and poach gently for about 4 minutes, or until the fish is just tender. Lift the fish out carefully with draining spoons and divide between the two gratin dishes, mixing with the prawns.

**4** Reduce the cooking liquor to 200 ml (7 fl oz), pour off and reserve. Rinse out the pan. Melt 25 g (1 oz) Clover, stir in the flour and cook for about 30 seconds. Blend in the cooking liquor gradually and bring to the boil, stirring all the time. Cook for 1–2 minutes, then remove from the heat and stir in the cream. Adjust seasoning; pour the sauce over the fish.

**5** Sprinkle grated cheese over the sauce and potatoes then stand the dishes on an edged baking sheet. Bake at 200°C (400°F) mark 6 for 25–30 minutes, or until golden and bubbling. Garnish with dill or parsley.

# MACKEREL FILLETS IN OATMEAL AND ALMONDS

**SERVES 4**
*Preparation time: 20 minutes*
*Cooking time: 10 minutes*

| |
|---|
| 2 whole mackerel, about 550 g (1¼ lb) each, cleaned |
| 30 ml (2 tbsp) plain flour, seasoned with salt and pepper |
| 75 g (3 oz) whole almonds |
| 100 g (4 oz) coarse oatmeal |
| 1 egg, lightly beaten |
| 1 orange |
| spinach or watercress and orange salad, to accompany |

**1** Cut the heads off the mackerel, then, using a sharp knife, split the fish open all the way along the underside.

**2** Place the fish flesh-side down on a board and press firmly all along the backbone to loosen the bone and flatten the fish. Turn the fish flesh-side up and ease out the bones.

**3** Cut each fish in half to give two fillets then, if wished, carefully skin each one (this may be difficult if the fish is really fresh). Coat each fillet lightly in the seasoned flour.

**4** Blanch the almonds in boiling water for about 1 minute. Pop them out of their skins and finely chop. Place in a shallow dish with the oatmeal.

**5** Dip each fillet of mackerel into the egg, then coat in the nuts and oatmeal. Place on a baking sheet.

**6** Squeeze a little orange juice over each fillet, then place under a hot grill and cook for about 5 minutes on each side. Serve immediately, accompanied by a spinach or watercress and orange salad.

*Left:  Gratin of Seafood (page 55)*
*Centre:  Salad Niçoise (page 63)*
*Right:  Poached Plaice and Spinach Flan (page 62)*

# SALMON FILLET EN CROÛTE

### SERVES 4
*Preparation time: 30 minutes plus 15 minutes chilling*
*Cooking time: 45 minutes*

| |
|---|
| *plain flour* |
| *100 g (4 oz) Gruyère cheese, finely grated* |
| *115 g (4½ oz) Clover* |
| *1.25 ml (¼ tsp) cayenne pepper* |
| *1 egg yolk plus 1 egg* |
| *25 g (1 oz) long-grain rice* |
| *salt and pepper* |
| *30 ml (2 tbsp) chopped fresh parsley* |
| *10 ml (2 tsp) chopped fresh dill or 5 ml (1 tsp) dried dill* |
| *50 ml (2 fl oz) milk* |
| *30 ml (2 tbsp) soured cream* |
| *1 lemon* |
| *two 125 g (4 oz) salmon fillets, skinned* |
| *clarified butter, chopped dill and steamed cucumber, to serve* |

**1** Rub together 100 g (4 oz) flour, cheese, 100 g (4 oz) Clover and cayenne pepper. Add the egg yolk and 15 ml (1 tbsp) water to bind to a soft dough. Knead lightly until quite smooth. Wrap; chill for 15 minutes.

**2** Cook the rice in plenty of boiling salted water. Drain well and stir in the parsley, dill and seasoning.

**3** Melt the remaining 15 g (½ oz) Clover in a small saucepan. Stir in 15 g (½ oz) flour, the milk, soured cream and grated lemon rind. Bring to the boil and beat well until thickened. Cool.

**4** On a lightly floured surface, roll the dough out to a 20.5 cm (8 inch) square. Keep the dough well floured and moving while rolling. Place on a flat baking sheet.

**5** Place one salmon fillet in the centre of the bottom half of the pastry. Spread with half the sauce mixture. Spoon on the rice and dot the remaining sauce over the top. Finish with the remaining salmon fillet.

**6** Brush the edges of the pastry lightly with the beaten egg. Fold the top half over the salmon to enclose. Press the edges together to seal. Trim off any excess pastry.

**7** Brush all over with beaten egg. Lightly score with a knife in a crisscross pattern. Bake at 200°C (400°F) mark 6 for about 30 minutes. Serve hot with clarified butter, chopped dill and steamed cucumber, or cold with a generous mixed leaf salad.

# HALIBUT WITH WINE AND TOMATOES

### SERVES 6
*Preparation time: 20 minutes*
*Cooking time: 40 minutes*

| |
|---|
| *150 ml (¼ pint) medium dry white wine* |
| *175 g (6 oz) onion, skinned and finely chopped* |
| *175 g (6 oz) mushrooms, wiped and quartered* |
| *15 g (½ oz) fresh root ginger, peeled and finely chopped* |
| *40 g (1½ oz) Clover* |
| *45 ml (3 tbsp) plain flour* |
| *450 g (1 lb) ripe tomatoes, skinned and roughly chopped* |
| *15 ml (1 tbsp) tomato purée* |
| *salt and pepper* |
| *3 large or 6 small halibut or cod steaks, about 900 g (2 lb) total weight* |

**1** Heat the Clover in a frying pan; add the onion and ginger and cook over a gentle heat for about 5 minutes, stirring occasionally. Stir in 30 ml (2 tbsp) flour followed by the wine, tomatoes, mushrooms, tomato purée and seasoning. Bring to the boil, cook for 2 minutes, take off the heat and cool slightly.

**2** Meanwhile, carefully ease the skin off the fish. Rinse and dry the steaks, coat with remaining flour, then place in a shallow ovenproof dish which will take the fish in a single layer. Spoon over the tomato sauce.

**3** Cover the dish tightly and place on the top shelf in the oven. Bake at 180°C (350°F) mark 4 for about 30 minutes or until the fish eases away from the bone when tested with a sharp knife.

# MUSSELS IN TOMATO SAUCE

**SERVES 2**
*Preparation time: 30 minutes plus overnight*
*Cooking time: 20 minutes*

| |
|---|
| 1.1 kg (2½ lb) or 2.8 litres (5 pints) fresh mussels |
| salt and pepper |
| 40 g (1½ oz) coarse oatmeal |
| 1 medium onion, skinned and chopped |
| 25 g (1 oz) Clover |
| 1 clove garlic, skinned and crushed |
| 5 ml (1 tsp) dried thyme |
| 450 g (1 lb) ripe tomatoes, skinned, deseeded and roughly chopped |
| 15 ml (1 tbsp) tomato purée |
| 5 ml (1 tsp) white wine vinegar |
| 300 ml (½ pint) dry cider |
| 15 ml (1 tbsp) fresh chopped parsley |

**1** Pick over the mussels, discarding any that have opened or damaged shells. Scrub the shells under cold running water to remove any sand or grit. Then, using a small knife, trim away the beard (the weed caught between the closed shells) and scrape off any barnacles.

**2** Place the prepared mussels in a large bowl, cover with cold salted water and sprinkle over the oatmeal. Leave in a cool place overnight, then wash and drain well. Check all mussels are still tightly closed.

**3** Heat the Clover in a large saucepan and add the onion, garlic and thyme. Cook, stirring, for 1–2 minutes, then stir in the tomatoes and any juices, the tomato purée, vinegar, seasoning and cider. Add the mussels, bring to the boil, cover tightly and cook over a moderate heat for 5–7 minutes, shaking the pan occasionally, until all the shells are open.

**4** Using a slotted spoon, transfer the mussels to a warmed serving dish, discarding any unopened shells. Cover with foil to keep the mussels warm.

**5** Bring the cooking liquor back to the boil and boil rapidly for 1–2 minutes. Adjust seasoning then pour over the mussels. Garnish with the chopped parsley.

# POTATO-TOPPED FISH PIE

**SERVES 4**
*Preparation time: 30 minutes*
*Cooking time: 1 hour*

| |
|---|
| 450 g (1 lb) celeriac, peeled and cut into chunks |
| 700 g (1½ lb) potatoes, peeled and cut into chunks |
| salt and pepper |
| 700 g (1½ lb) whiting, cod or haddock fillet |
| 150 ml (¼ pint) milk |
| bay leaves and peppercorns for flavouring |
| 25 g (1 oz) Clover |
| 100 g (4 oz) courgettes, trimmed and thinly sliced |
| 30 ml (2 tbsp) plain flour |
| 75 g (3 oz) button mushrooms, wiped and halved |
| 45 ml (3 tbsp) Greek-style yogurt |

**1** Boil the celeriac and potatoes together in salted water until tender. Drain.

**2** Place the fish in a sauté pan, pour over the milk and 150 ml (¼ pint) water. Add the flavouring ingredients, cover and poach for about 10 minutes or until just tender.

**3** Using a fish slice, remove fish from the pan and flake into large pieces, discarding any skin and bones. Strain the liquor into a jug. Reserve.

**4** Rinse the sauté pan, melt the Clover, add the courgettes and cook for 1–2 minutes. Mix in the flour and cook for a further 2–3 minutes.

**5** Stir in the reserved liquor, bring to the boil then boil for 1–2 minutes or until thickened. Add the mushrooms and fish and adjust seasoning. Pour into a 1.6 litre (2¾ pint) pie dish.

**6** Mash the celeriac and potatoes until smooth. Beat in the yogurt, then season to taste. Spoon on top of the fish, smoothing over the surface.

**7** Place the dish on a baking sheet and bake at 200°C (400°F) mark 6 for about 25 minutes or until golden and bubbling.

# GOLDEN FISH LASAGNE

**SERVES 8**
*Preparation time: 25 minutes*
*Cooking time: 55 minutes*

350 g (12 oz) fresh haddock fillet

350 g (12 oz) smoked haddock fillet

1.1 litre (2 pints) milk

2 bay leaves

slices of onion and carrot

salt and pepper

vegetable oil

350 g (12 oz) lasagne

225 g (8 oz) button mushrooms, wiped and sliced

90 g (3½ oz) Clover

75 g (3 oz) flour

150 g (5 oz) carton soft cheese

45 ml (3 tbsp) chopped fresh parsley

30 ml (2 tbsp) sherry

100 g (4 oz) cooked peeled prawns

100 g (4 oz) Cheddar cheese, grated

**1** Place the haddock fillets in a large frying or sauté pan. Pour over half the milk and add the bay leaves and slices of onion and carrot. Bring slowly to the boil, cover and simmer until the fish flakes. Cool slightly. Strain off milk; reserve. Flake fish.

**2** Bring two large pans of salted water to the boil. Add a dash of oil and half the lasagne to each. Boil gently for about 12 minutes or until the lasagne is just tender, then drain and rinse under the cold tap. Immediately spread out on absorbent kitchen paper to drain. Cover with another layer of paper, leave only 10 minutes.

**3** Meanwhile, melt the Clover, in a large saucepan. Stir in the flour and cook for 1 minute, stirring all the time. Off the heat, add the strained milk and remaining fresh milk. Bring to the boil, stirring frequently, and cook for 2 minutes. Remove from the heat, stir in the soft cheese, parsley, sherry, mushrooms, flaked fish and prawns. Season well.

**4** Lightly grease a 3.1 litre (5½ pint) shallow ovenproof dish. Layer up the pasta and sauce, beginning and ending with sauce. Top with the grated cheese.

**5** Stand on a baking sheet and bake at 200°C (400°F) mark 6 for 30 minutes, or until golden and bubbling.

# TROUT POACHED IN WINE

**SERVES 4**
*Preparation time: 15 minutes*
*Cooking time: 35 minutes*

4 whole small trout, cleaned

salt and pepper

50 g (2 oz) butter or Clover

1 large onion, skinned and sliced

2 celery sticks, trimmed and sliced

2 carrots, peeled and very thinly sliced

300 ml (½ pint) dry white wine

bouquet garni

15 ml (1 tbsp) plain flour

lemon wedges and chopped fresh parsley, to garnish

**1** Wash the trout under cold running water and drain. Pat dry and season the insides.

**2** Melt 25 g (1 oz) of the butter or Clover in a small saucepan. Add the onion, celery and carrots and stir well to coat with butter or Clover. Cover and sweat for 5 minutes.

**3** Lay the vegetables in a greased casserole and arrange the fish on top. Pour over wine and add bouquet garni.

**4** Cover tightly and cook in the oven at 180°C (350°F) mark 4 for about 25 minutes until the trout are cooked.

**5** Transfer to a warmed serving dish and keep hot.

**6** Pour the cooking juices into a small pan, discarding the bouquet garni. Blend together the remaining butter or Clover and the flour. Whisk into the sauce and simmer gently, stirring, until thickened. Pour into a sauceboat or jug. Garnish with lemon and parsley.

*Right: Trout Poached in Wine*

# POACHED PLAICE AND SPINACH FLAN

### SERVES 4
*Preparation time: 25 minutes plus 15 minutes chilling*
*Cooking time: 55 minutes*

| |
| --- |
| 100 g (4 oz) butter or Clover |
| 175 g (6 oz) plain white flour |
| salt and pepper |
| 2 small eggs, beaten |
| 2 medium plaice, skinned and filleted, about 450 g (1 lb) filleted weight |
| 300 ml (½ pint) milk |
| few black peppercorns |
| 1 bay leaf |
| 100 g (4 oz) fresh spinach or 50 g (2 oz) frozen chopped spinach |
| 50 g (2 oz) Brie |
| 15 ml (1 tbsp) freshly grated Parmesan cheese |

1 Rub 75 g (3 oz) of butter or Clover into 175 g (6 oz) of flour with the salt until the mixture resembles breadcrumbs. Add enough water to make a soft dough. Turn out onto a floured surface and knead lightly together.

2 Roll out the pastry on a lightly floured surface and line a 34 × 11 cm (13½ × 4½ inch) loose-based, fluted tranche tin. Chill for 10–15 minutes. Place tin on a flat baking sheet and bake blind for about 20 minutes or until just cooked through.

3 Meanwhile, halve the plaice fillets lengthways to make 8 fillets. Roll up skinned side in. Place in a saucepan into which they will just fit and pour over the milk. Add the peppercorns and bay leaf. Cover and bring slowly to the boil, simmer for about 2 minutes or until fillets are just cooked. Remove with a slotted spoon then dry on absorbent kitchen paper. Strain and reserve liquid.

4 If using fresh spinach, wash, trim and, without drying it, place in a medium-sized saucepan. Cover and cook over a gentle heat for 3–4 minutes or until wilted. Drain well. Squeeze out any liquid and chop.

5 Melt the remaining butter or Clover in a medium saucepan. Stir in the flour and cook, stirring, for 1–2 minutes before adding 200 ml (7 fl oz) of the reserved poaching liquid. Season and bring to the boil. Simmer for 2–3 minutes until thickened and smooth. Off the heat, beat in the rinded and roughly chopped Brie, beaten eggs and spinach. Add frozen spinach at this stage, stirring until evenly blended.

6 Place the poached fish down the centre of the prepared flan tin. Spoon over the sauce. Sprinkle with the Parmesan.

7 Bake at 180°C (350°F) mark 4 for 25–30 minutes or until just set. Brown under a hot grill for 1–2 minutes. Serve warm.

# SKATE WITH CAPERS

### SERVES 4
*Preparation time: 5 minutes*
*Cooking time: 20 minutes*

| |
| --- |
| 700–900 g (1½–2 lb) wing of skate |
| salt |
| 50 g (2 oz) butter or Clover |
| 15 ml (1 tbsp) white wine vinegar |
| 10 ml (2 tsp) capers |
| 10 ml (2 tsp) chopped fresh parsley, to garnish |

1 Simmer the skate in a pan of salted water for 10–15 minutes until tender. Drain and keep warm.

2 Heat the butter or Clover in a pan until melted. Add the vinegar and capers, cook for a further 2–3 minutes and pour it over the fish. Serve at once, garnished with the parsley.

# STUFFED COD CRÊPES

### SERVES 6
### *Preparation time: 25 minutes*
### *Cooking time: 1 hour 15 minutes*

| |
|---|
| *175 g (6 oz) plus 45 ml (3 tbsp) plain flour* |
| *50 g (2 oz) salted peanuts, very finely chopped* |
| *2 eggs* |
| *15 ml (1 tbsp) vegetable oil* |
| *450 ml (¾ pint) milk and water mixed* |
| *700 g (1½ lb) cod fillet* |
| *568 ml (1 pint) milk* |
| *50 g (2 oz) butter* |
| *100 g (4 oz) celery, chopped* |
| *5 ml (1 tsp) curry powder* |
| *salt and pepper* |
| *75 ml (5 tbsp) single cream* |
| *50 g (2 oz) Cheddar cheese, grated* |
| *chopped fresh parsley, to garnish* |

1 Make the batter for the crêpes. Whisk 175 g (6 oz) flour, the chopped peanuts, eggs, oil and half the milk and water mixture until quite smooth. Whisk in the remaining liquid.

2 Lightly oil an 18 cm (7 inch) heavy frying pan. Spoon in about 30 ml (2 tbsp) batter, tipping the pan to spread the batter. Cook until golden underneath, then turn over and cook the other side. Make 12 pancakes.

3 Place the cod in a deep frying pan with the milk. Cover and poach gently for about 12 minutes until the fish is tender and begins to flake. Strain off and reserve the liquid. Flake the fish, discarding skin and bones.

4 Melt the butter or Clover in a heavy-based saucepan, add the celery and curry powder and fry gently for 1 minute, stirring. Remove from the heat and stir in the remaining flour, reserved fish liquid and season to taste. Bring to the boil, stirring, and simmer for 1 minute. Remove from the heat and fold in the cream and flaked fish.

5 Divide the filling between the crêpes, roll up and place side by side in a single layer in a greased shallow ovenproof dish. Sprinkle the grated cheese on top.

6 Cover with foil and bake in the oven at 180°C (350°F) mark 4 for about 40 minutes. Garnish with parsley.

# SALAD NIÇOISE

### SERVES 4
### *Preparation time: 25 minutes*
### *Cooking time: 15 minutes*

| |
|---|
| *175 g (6 oz) small new potatoes, scrubbed and halved* |
| *salt and pepper* |
| *90 ml (6 tbsp) olive oil* |
| *30 ml (2 tbsp) white wine vinegar* |
| *15 ml (1 tbsp) lemon juice* |
| *15 ml (1 tbsp) mild wholegrain mustard* |
| *large pinch of sugar* |
| *198 g (7 oz) can tuna fish, drained* |
| *225 g (8 oz) tomatoes, quartered* |
| *50 g (2 oz) black olives, stoned* |
| *½ small cucumber, thinly sliced* |
| *225 g (8 oz) cooked French beans* |
| *2 hard-boiled eggs, shelled and quartered* |
| *½ of an iceberg lettuce, cut into chunks* |
| *30 ml (2 tbsp) chopped fresh parsley* |
| *8 anchovy fillets, drained and halved* |
| *French bread, to serve* |

1 Cook the potatoes in boiling salted water until tender. Meanwhile, make the dressing by whisking together the oil, vinegar, lemon juice, mustard and sugar. Season generously with salt and pepper.

2 Drain the potatoes and toss in the dressing. Leave to cool, stirring occasionally.

3 Flake the tuna into large chunks. Arrange in a bowl with the tomatoes, olives, cucumber, beans, eggs, lettuce and cold potatoes. Sprinkle with anchovies and parsley.

Chapter 6

# ACCOMPANIMENTS

# PARSNIP CROQUETTES

**SERVES 4**
*Preparation time: 30 minutes plus 30 minutes chilling*
*Cooking time: 10 minutes*

| |
|---|
| 700 g (1½ lb) parsnips, peeled and cut into large chunks |
| salt and pepper |
| 50 g (2 oz) soft cheese |
| 1 egg plus 1 egg yolk |
| 100 g (4 oz) stale breadcrumbs |

**1** Cook the parsnips in boiling salted water until tender. Drain well, then return to the pan and cook over a high heat, stirring, until all of the water has evaporated.

**2** Mash or sieve the parsnips then beat in the cheese and egg yolk. Allow to cool.

**3** With floured hands, shape the mixture into dumpy logs, about 6.5 cm (2½ in) in length. Place on a baking sheet and chill for about 15 minutes or until firm.

**4** Coat the croquettes in lightly beaten egg, then breadcrumbs, and chill for a further 15 minutes.

**5** Place the baking sheet of croquettes under a hot grill and cook for about 7 minutes, turning frequently. Serve with casseroles and stews.

# SUMMER VEGETABLE FRICASSÉE

**SERVES 4–6**
*Preparation time: 20 minutes*
*Cooking time: 15 minutes*

| |
|---|
| 4 courgettes, washed and trimmed |
| 225 g (8 oz) French beans, topped and tailed and cut into 5 cm (2 inch) lengths |
| salt and pepper |
| 40 g (1½ oz) Clover |
| 1 onion, skinned and sliced |
| 2 cloves garlic, skinned and crushed |
| 5 ml (1 tsp) crushed coriander seeds |
| 3 peppers (red, yellow, green), cored, seeded and sliced |
| 150 ml (¼ pint) dry white wine |
| 10 ml (2 tsp) tomato purée |
| 2.5 ml (½ tsp) sugar |

**1** Cut the courgettes crossways into thirds, then cut them lengthways into slices about 0.5 cm (¼ inch) thick.

**2** Blanch the courgettes and beans in boiling salted water for 5 minutes only. Drain and set aside until required.

**3** Heat the Clover in a flameproof casserole, add the onion, garlic and coriander seeds and fry gently for 5 minutes until onion is soft.

**4** Add the pepper slices and fry gently for a further 5 minutes, stirring constantly. Stir in the wine, tomato purée and sugar, with salt and pepper to taste. Bring to the boil, then simmer for a few minutes, stirring all the time until the liquid begins to reduce.

**5** Add the courgettes and beans to the pan and stir gently to combine with the sauce. Heat through, taking care not to overcook the vegetables. Taste and adjust seasoning. Serve hot, straight from the casserole, with roast meat or baked fish.

# RED CABBAGE AND GARLIC

**SERVES 6**
*Preparation time: 20 minutes*
*Cooking time: 50 minutes*

*900 g (2 lb) red cabbage, thinly shredded*
*40 g (1½ oz) Clover*
*1 large onion, skinned and thinly sliced*
*1 clove garlic, skinned and crushed*
*juice of 1 large orange*
*salt and pepper*

1 Wash and drain the cabbage well.

2 Heat the Clover in a large saucepan, add the onion and garlic and cook for 2–3 minutes. Mix in the red cabbage and cook, stirring, for a further minute.

3 Pour in the strained juice from the orange; season.

4 Cover *tightly* and cook over a medium heat for about 45 minutes or until just tender. Stir occasionally. Adjust seasoning. Serve with roasts and braised dishes.

# SESAME MUSHROOMS

**SERVES 6**
*Preparation time: 10 minutes*
*Cooking time: 15 minutes*

*700 g (1½ lb) button mushrooms*
*40 g (1½ oz) Clover*
*15 ml (1 tbsp) soy sauce*
*30 ml (2 tbsp) sesame seeds*
*60 ml (4 tbsp) medium sherry*
*salt and pepper*
*30 ml (2 tbsp) chopped fresh parsley*

1 Wipe the mushrooms, halving any large ones. Heat the Clover and soy sauce together in a large sauté pan. Add the mushrooms and cook over a high heat for 2–3 minutes, stirring.

2 Sprinkle the sesame seeds over the mushrooms and add the sherry. Bring the mixture slowly to the boil, cover and cook for about 2–3 minutes.

3 Uncover and boil rapidly until the liquid is reduced by half. Adjust seasoning and garnish with the chopped parsley. Serve with grilled meats and chops.

# STIR-FRIED CABBAGE WITH WALNUTS

**SERVES 4**
*Preparation time: 20 minutes*
*Cooking time: 10 minutes*

*700 g (1½ lb) Savoy or winter cabbage, coarsely shredded*
*40 g (1½ oz) Clover*
*1 clove garlic, skinned and crushed*
*450 g (1 lb) carrots, pared and cut into thin, flat strips*
*grated rind and juice of 1 lime*
*20 ml (4 tsp) soy sauce*
*45 ml (3 tbsp) stock*
*50 g (2 oz) walnuts*
*salt and pepper*

1 Wash and drain the cabbage well.

2 Heat the Clover in a wok or large frying pan, add the crushed garlic with carrot slices and cook, stirring, for 2–3 minutes, or until the carrots are beginning to soften.

3 Mix the cabbage, rind and juice of the lime, soy sauce and stock. Cook, stirring all the time, for a further 2–3 minutes, or until the cabbage is just cooked. Add the walnuts and season. Serve with casseroles.

# JERUSALEM ARTICHOKES IN MUSTARD SAUCE

**SERVES 4**
*Preparation time: 15 minutes*
*Cooking time: 20 minutes*

| |
|---|
| 1.1 kg (2½ lb) Jerusalem artichokes, peeled |
| 350 ml (12 fl oz) milk |
| 25 g (1 oz) butter or Clover |
| 30 ml (2 tbsp) flour |
| 10 ml (2 tsp) wholegrain mustard |
| salt and pepper |

**1** Cut any large artichokes in half. Place in a saucepan with the milk and bring to the boil. Reduce heat, cover and simmer until the artichokes are just tender. Drain well, reserving the liquor. Place the artichokes in a serving dish and keep warm, covered.

**2** Melt the butter or Clover in a saucepan, add the flour and cook for 1–2 minutes. Stir in the reserved milk, bring to the boil and boil, stirring, until thickened. Stir in the mustard and season.

**3** Pour the sauce over the artichokes and serve immediately with grilled steak or roast beef.

# AUBERGINE AND PEPPER SALAD

**SERVES 4**
*Preparation time: 20 minutes*
*Cooking time: 20 minutes*

| |
|---|
| 3 small aubergines, about 700 g (1½ lb) total weight |
| 1 red pepper, about 225 g (8 oz) |
| 1 green pepper, about 225 g (8 oz) |
| 175 g (6 oz) slice fresh white bread |
| 90 ml (6 tbsp) olive oil |
| 30 ml (2 tbsp) red wine vinegar |
| salt and pepper |
| 60 ml (4 tbsp) chopped fresh oregano or 20 ml (4 tsp) dried |

**1** Make 2 or 3 long slits in the skin of each aubergine. Place under a hot grill with the peppers and grill until the skins begin to blacken and peel away. The aubergines must feel very soft; leave them under the grill for 15–20 minutes.

**2** Cool slightly before peeling away the skins. Cube the aubergines and peppers and arrange on a flat serving dish.

**3** Lightly toast the bread, cut into cubes and scatter over the salad.

**4** Mix together the oil, vinegar, seasoning and oregano. Drizzle over the salad. Serve warm or cold with grilled or barbecued lamb or sausages.

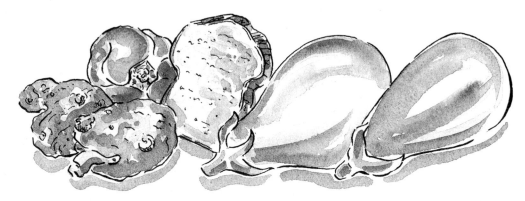

Left: *Aubergine and Pepper Salad (page 67)*
Centre: *Sesame Mushrooms (page 66)*
Right: *Parsnip Croquettes (page 65)*

# MUSHROOM AND HAM RISOTTO

**SERVES 4**
*Preparation time: 10 minutes*
*Cooking time: 55 minutes*

| |
|---|
| 90 g (3½ oz) butter or Clover |
| 15 ml (1 tbsp) olive oil |
| 2 small onions, skinned and finely chopped |
| 1 clove garlic, skinned and crushed |
| 225 g (8 oz) mushrooms, sliced |
| 30 ml (2 tbsp) chopped fresh parsley |
| 900 ml (1½ pints) chicken stock |
| 350 g (12 oz) risotto rice |
| 150 ml (¼ pint) white wine |
| 50 g (2 oz) cooked ham, diced |
| 25 g (1 oz) freshly grated Parmesan cheese |
| salt and pepper |

**1** Melt 15 g (½ oz) butter or Clover and 15 ml (1 tbsp) olive oil in a saucepan. Add half the onion and fry gently for 5 minutes until soft but not coloured.

**2** Add the garlic, cook for 1 minute, then add the mushrooms and parsley. Cook gently for 10 minutes until the mushrooms are tender. Stir in 25 g (1 oz) butter or Clover and set aside while making the risotto.

**3** Bring the stock to the boil in a large saucepan and keep at barely simmering point.

**4** In a large, heavy-based saucepan, melt 25 g (1 oz) butter, add the rest of the onion and fry gently for 5 minutes until soft but not coloured.

**5** Add the rice and stir well for 2–3 minutes until the rice is well coated with the butter.

**6** Add the wine, cook gently, stirring until absorbed. Add 150 ml (¼ pint) of stock as soon as the wine is absorbed. Continue to add stock in 150 ml (¼ pint) measures, stirring frequently until the risotto is thick and creamy, tender but not sticky. This should take 20–25 minutes. It must not be hurried.

**7** Finally, stir in the remaining butter or Clover, ham, mushroom mixture and cheese. Taste and adjust seasoning. Serve immediately with grilled meats.

# GRUYÈRE POTATOES

**SERVES 6**
*Preparation time: 20 minutes*
*Cooking time: 2 hours*

| |
|---|
| 900 g (2 lb) potatoes, peeled and thinly sliced (do not soak in cold water) |
| 25 g (1 oz) butter or Clover |
| 100 g (4 oz) Gruyère cheese, grated |
| freshly grated nutmeg |
| salt and pepper |
| 568 ml (1 pint) milk |

**1** Use a little of the butter or Clover to lightly grease a 1.4 litre (2½ pint) shallow ovenproof dish.

**2** Layer the potatoes and most of the cheese in the dish. Add a generous grating of nutmeg, and season to taste.

**3** Top with cheese and then pour over the milk, which should just cover the potatoes.

**4** Dot the surface with the remaining butter or Clover. Cover with foil and bake in the oven at 180°C (350°F) mark 4 for about 1½–2 hours, or until the potatoes are quite tender and most of the milk has been absorbed. Remove the foil half an hour before the end of the cooking time so the top gets golden brown. Serve with roast meats or grilled fish.

# Chapter 7

# _Desserts_

*Left:  Chocolate and Lime Mousse (page 83)*
*Centre:  Raspberry Walnut Torte (page 74)*
*Right:  Meringue Basket (page 79)*

# RASPBERRY WALNUT TORTE

**SERVES 8**
*Preparation time: 45 minutes*
*Cooking time: 30 minutes*

| |
|---|
| 100 g (4 oz) walnuts |
| 100 g (4 oz) butter or Clover |
| 75 g (3 oz) caster sugar |
| 175 g (6 oz) plain flour |
| 450 g (1 lb) fresh raspberries |
| 50 g (2 oz) icing sugar |
| 30 ml (2 tbsp) raspberry-flavoured liqueur or kirsch (optional) |
| 300 ml (10 fl oz) double cream |
| 150 ml (5 fl oz) single cream |

**1** Grind the walnuts finely in a mouli grater, electric blender or food processor.

**2** Cream the butter or Clover and sugar together until light and fluffy, then beat in the walnuts and flour. Divide the dough into three.

**3** Draw three 20.5 cm (8 inch) circles on non-stick baking parchment. Place these on baking sheets.

**4** Put a piece of dough in the centre of each circle and press with the heel of your hand until the dough is the same size as the circle.

**5** Cut one of the circles into eight triangles with a sharp knife and ease them slightly apart. Refrigerate the pastries for 30 minutes. Bake in the oven at 190°C (375°F) mark 5 for 15–20 minutes, swapping over the sheets to ensure the pastries brown evenly. Leave to cool and harden for 10 minutes on the paper, then transfer to wire racks to cool completely.

**6** Meanwhile, reserve one third of the whole raspberries for decoration. Put the rest in a bowl with the icing sugar and liqueur, if using. Crush the fruit with a fork; leave to macerate while the pastry cools.

**7** Assemble the torte just before serving. Whip the creams together until thick, then fold in the crushed raspberries and juice. Stand one round of pastry on a flat serving plate and spread with half of the cream mixture. Top with remaining pastry and cream mixture.

**8** Arrange the triangles of pastry on top of the cream, wedging them in at an angle. Scatter the reserved whole raspberries between. Serve as soon as possible.

# WALNUT PEAR SLICE

**SERVES 6**
*Preparation time: 30 minutes plus 30 minutes chilling*
*Cooking time: 30 minutes*

| |
|---|
| 150 g (5 oz) plain white flour |
| ground cinnamon |
| 25 g (1 oz) ground walnuts |
| 1 lemon |
| 1 egg, lightly beaten |
| caster sugar |
| 50 g (2 oz) softened butter or Clover |
| 45 ml (3 tbsp) fresh brown breadcrumbs |
| 3 ripe pears |

**1** Sift the flour with 2.5 ml (½ tsp) ground cinnamon on to a clean dry work surface. Sprinkle the walnuts and grated rind of half the lemon over the flour. Make a well in the centre and into this place the egg, 50 g (2 oz) caster sugar and the butter or Clover.

**2** With the fingertips of one hand only, pinch the ingredients from the well together until evenly blended. Draw in the flour gradually, with the help of a palette knife; knead until smooth. Wrap and chill for about 30 minutes.

**3** Roll out the pastry to an oblong about 30.5 × 10 cm (12 × 4 inches), trimming the edges. Lift the pastry on to a baking sheet; sprinkle over the breadcrumbs.

**4** Peel, quarter and core each pear; slice each quarter into four or five pieces; toss gently in a little lemon juice. Drain and arrange in overlapping lines across the dough. Sprinkle over a little sugar and cinnamon.

**5** Bake at 190°C (375°F) mark 5 for about 30 minutes or until the pastry is well browned and crisp around the edges. Allow to cool slightly. Cut into slices; serve topped with cream or yogurt.

# GLAZED NUT FLAN

### SERVES 6–8
**_Preparation time: 25 minutes plus 1 hour chilling_**
**_Cooking time: 55 minutes_**

| |
|---|
| 2 egg yolks and 1 egg |
| 75 g (3 oz) softened butter or Clover |
| few drops vanilla essence |
| 75 g (3 oz) caster sugar |
| 100 g (4 oz) plus 15 ml (1 tbsp) plain white flour |
| 50 g (2 oz) hazelnuts |
| 25 g (1 oz) shelled pistachio nuts |
| 1 lemon |
| pinch grated nutmeg |
| 60 ml (4 tbsp) golden syrup |
| 75 g (3 oz) walnut pieces |
| 75 g (3 oz) Brazil nuts |
| 50 g (2 oz) pecan nuts |

**1** In a medium bowl, cream together two of the egg yolks, 50 g (2 oz) of the butter or Clover, the vanilla essence and 50 g (2 oz) of the sugar until smooth. Add the 100 g (4 oz) flour and stir quickly together with a large metal spoon. Turn out on to a floured surface and knead lightly together. Wrap in foil or cling film and chill for 20–25 minutes.

**2** Roll out the pastry on a lightly floured surface and line a 21.5 cm (8½ inch) loose-based fluted flan tin. Chill for 10–15 minutes.

**3** Place the flan tin on a baking sheet and bake blind until very lightly browned.

**4** Meanwhile, brown the hazelnuts under a hot grill. Place in a clean tea towel and rub well to remove the skins. Dip the pistachio nuts in boiling water for 1 minute. Drain and remove the skins; dry on absorbent kitchen paper.

**5** Melt the remaining butter or Clover; grate the lemon rind. With an electric whisk beat the egg and remaining sugar together for about 5 minutes or until very thick and pale. Quickly stir in the melted butter, lemon rind, nutmeg and 30 ml (2 tbsp) golden syrup. Fold in the remaining flour and finally all the nuts.

**6** Spoon the nut mixture into the prepared flan case. Bake at 180°C (350°F) mark 4 for about 35 minutes or until golden brown and firm to the touch; cool for 10–15 minutes.

**7** Heat together the remaining golden syrup and 30 ml (2 tbsp) lemon juice. Boil for 2–3 minutes until syrupy. Brush over the warm flan. Leave in the tin for 10–15 minutes before removing to a wire rack to cool. Serve warm or cold.

*Strawberry Custard Tart (page 78)*

# STRAWBERRY CUSTARD TART

SERVES 6–8
*Preparation time: 30 minutes plus 2 hours chilling*
*Cooking time: 25 minutes*

| |
|---|
| *175 g (6 oz) plain flour* |
| *100 g (4 oz) caster sugar* |
| *100 g (4 oz) butter or Clover* |
| *3 eggs* |
| *40 g (1½ oz) cornflour* |
| *450 ml (¾ pint) milk* |
| *few drops of vanilla flavouring* |
| *350 g (12 oz) strawberries, hulled* |
| *pouring cream, to serve* |

**1** Mix the flour with 25 g (1 oz) sugar in a bowl, then rub in the butter or Clover until the mixture resembles fine breadcrumbs. Bind to a soft dough with one egg. Knead lightly on a floured surface until just smooth.

**3** Roll out the pastry on a floured work surface and use to line a 23 cm (9 inch) flan dish. Refrigerate for 30 minutes. Prick the base of the flan and bake blind in the oven at 200°C (400°F) mark 6 for 20 minutes or until pale golden and cooked through. Cool in the dish for 30–40 minutes.

**3** Mix the cornflour to a smooth paste with a little of the milk. Separate the remaining eggs and mix the egg yolks with the cornflour paste. Put the rest of the milk in a saucepan with the remaining sugar and the vanilla flavouring. Bring to the boil, then remove from the heat and pour in the cornflour mixture. Return to the boil, stirring, and boil for 2 minutes until thickened. Cover with damp greaseproof paper and cool for 30 minutes. (Whisk if necessary to remove lumps.)

**4** Thinly slice the strawberries into the base of the flan, reserving a few for decoration. Whisk the egg whites until stiff and fold into the cold custard mixture. Smooth the custard mixture evenly over the strawberries. Refrigerate for 1 hour until set.

**5** Serve the flan decorated with the reserved strawberries, preferably within 2 hours. Serve with cream.

# STEAMED COCONUT SPONGE WITH ORANGE CUSTARD

SERVES 6–8
*Preparation time: 15 minutes*
*Cooking time: 2 hours*

| |
|---|
| *175 g (6 oz) butter or Clover* |
| *75 g (3 oz) dark soft brown sugar* |
| *caster sugar* |
| *6 large oranges* |
| *3 eggs, beaten* |
| *50 g (2 oz) desiccated coconut* |
| *225 g (8 oz) self-raising white flour* |
| *30 ml (2 tbsp) custard powder* |
| *450 ml (¾ pint) milk* |

**1** Grease and base-line a 1.4 litre (2½ pint) pudding basin. Put a large pan of water on to boil over which a steamer will fit.

**2** Beat together the butter or Clover, brown sugar, 75 g (3 oz) caster sugar and the finely grated rind of one orange until light and fluffy. Gradually beat in the eggs, keeping the mixture stiff. Gently fold in the coconut, flour and 45 ml (3 tbsp) orange juice. Spoon into the prepared bowl then cover with pleated and greased greaseproof paper and foil. Tie down securely. Place the bowl in the steamer; cover and steam for about 2 hours.

**3** Meanwhile, prepare the custard. Mix the powder to a smooth paste with 30 ml (2 tbsp) caster sugar and a little milk. Heat the remaining milk, then stir into the powder mixture. Return to the pan and bring to the boil, stirring all the time; cook for 1–2 minutes. Pour out into a bowl and cool slightly, then whisk in about 150 ml (¼ pint) orange juice. Leave to cool further, whisking occasionally.

**4** Using a serrated knife, cut all peel and pith from remaining oranges. Slice the flesh, discarding pips.

**5** Turn out the pudding to serve with the orange custard and slices of fresh orange.

# Meringue Basket

**SERVES 6–8**
*Preparation time: 30 minutes*
*Cooking time: 5 hours*

*4 egg whites*
*225 g (8 oz) icing sugar*
*300 ml (10 fl oz) whipping cream*
*30 ml (2 tbsp) kirsch*
*prepared fruit in season, such as strawberries, raspberries, star fruit, grapes, redcurrants*

**1** Line three baking sheets with non-stick baking parchment and draw a 19 cm (7½ inch) circle on each. Turn the paper over so that the pencilled circle is visible but does not mark the meringues.

**2** Place 3 egg whites in a clean, dry, heatproof bowl, and place the bowl over a pan of simmering water. Sift in 175 g (6 oz) of the icing sugar.

**3** Whisk the egg whites and sugar vigorously over the simmering water until the mixture stands in very stiff peaks. Do not allow the bowl to get too hot.

**4** Fit a piping bag with a large star nozzle. Spoon in one third of the meringue mixture. Secure the paper to the baking sheets with a little meringue.

**5** Pipe two rings of meringue about 1 cm (½ inch) thick inside the circles on two of the sheets of baking paper.

**6** Fill the bag with the remaining meringue and, starting from the centre, pipe a continuous coil of meringue for a solid base on the third sheet of paper. Place all in the oven at 100°C (200°F) gas mark LOW for 2½–3 hours to dry out.

**7** Use the remaining egg white and sugar to make meringue as before and put into the piping bag. Remove the cooked meringue rings from the paper and layer them up on the base, piping a ring of fresh meringue between each. (This will create a more solid case for the fruit and cream.) Return to the oven for a further 1½–2 hours. Slide on to a wire rack and peel off base paper when cool.

**8** Just before serving, stand the meringue shell on a flat serving plate. Lightly whip the cream and fold in the kirsch; spoon half into the base of the basket and top with half the fruit. Whirl the remaining cream over the top and decorate with the remaining fruit.

# Spiced Bread and Butter Pudding

**SERVES 4**
*Preparation time: 20 minutes*
*Cooking time: 1 hour*

*225 g (8 oz) fruited batch loaf*
*50 g (2 oz) butter or Clover*
*30 ml (2 tbsp) soft brown sugar*
*75 g (3 oz) sultanas*
*5 ml (1 tsp) ground cinnamon*
*grated rind of 1 orange*
*3 eggs*
*568 ml (1 pint) milk*
*icing sugar, to decorate*

**1** Thinly slice the fruit loaf, then spread each slice with a little butter or Clover; reserve the remainder.

**2** Mix together the sugar, sultanas, cinnamon and orange rind. Arrange a few slices of the fruit loaf in a shallow, well-greased 1.3 litre (2¼ pint) ovenproof dish. Sprinkle over the sugar mixture then add another layer of fruit loaf.

**3** In a jug whisk together the eggs and milk, pour over the pudding and dot the surface with the remaining butter or Clover.

**4** Bake at 180°C (350°F) mark 4 for about 1 hour or until the pudding is firm to the touch and well browned. Dust with icing sugar if wished.

*Walnut Pear Slice (page 74)*

*Baked Alaska (page 83)*

# CHOCOLATE COFFEE REFRIGERATOR SLICE

**SERVES 6–8**
*Preparation time: 30 minutes plus 2–3 hours chilling*

| |
|---|
| 30 ml (2 tbsp) instant coffee granules |
| 45 ml (3 tbsp) brandy |
| 100 g (4 oz) plain chocolate |
| 100 g (4 oz) butter or Clover |
| 50 g (2 oz) icing sugar |
| 2 egg yolks |
| 300 ml (10 fl oz) whipping cream |
| 50 g (2 oz) chopped almonds, toasted |
| about 30 boudoir biscuits (sponge fingers) |

**1** Make up the coffee granules with 200 ml (7 fl oz) boiling water and stir in the brandy: cool.

**2** Break up the chocolate and melt in a small basin with 15 ml (1 tbsp) boiling water: cool.

**3** Whisk the butter or Clover and icing sugar together until pale and fluffy. Add the egg yolks, beating well.

**4** Stir in the cooled chocolate. Whip the fresh cream until softly stiff and stir half into the chocolate mixture, with the nuts. Refrigerate the remaining fresh cream.

**5** Butter and base-line a 21.5 × 11.5 cm (8½ × 4½ inch) top measurement loaf tin with non-stick paper and line the bottom with sponge fingers, cutting to fit if necessary. Spoon over a third of the coffee mixture.

**6** Layer up the tin with the chocolate mixture and sponge fingers, soaking each layer with coffee, and ending up with soaked sponge fingers. Weight down lightly and refrigerate for several hours.

**7** Turn out on to serving dish. Decorate with remaining whipped cream.

# HOT CHOCOLATE CHEESECAKE

**SERVES 8–10**
*Preparation time: 20 minutes plus 30 minutes chilling*
*Cooking time: 1 hour 45 minutes*

| |
|---|
| 100 g (4 oz) butter or Clover, melted |
| 225 g (8 oz) chocolate digestive biscuits, crushed |
| 2 eggs, separated |
| 75 g (3 oz) caster sugar |
| 225 g (8 oz) curd cheese |
| 40 g (1½ oz) ground or very finely chopped hazelnuts |
| 150 ml (5 fl oz) double cream |
| 25 g (1 oz) cocoa powder |
| 10 ml (2 tsp) dark rum |
| icing sugar, to finish |

**1** Stir the melted butter or Clover into the crushed biscuits and mix well, then press into the base and 4 cm (1½ inches) up the sides of a 20 cm (8 inch) loose-bottomed cake tin. Refrigerate for 30 minutes.

**2** Whisk the egg yolks and sugar together until thick enough to leave a trail on the surface when the whisk is lifted.

**3** Whisk in the cheese, nuts, cream, cocoa powder and rum until evenly blended.

**4** Whisk the egg whites until stiff, then fold into the cheese mixture. Pour into the biscuit base then bake in a preheated oven at 170°C (325°F) mark 3 for 1½–1¾ hours until risen.

**5** Remove carefully from the tin. Sift the icing sugar over the top to coat lightly and serve immediately while still hot.

# Chocolate and Lime Mousse

### SERVES 2
*Preparation time: 30 minutes plus 2 hours chilling*

| |
|---|
| 75 g (3 oz) plain chocolate |
| 2 eggs, separated |
| 15 ml (1 tbsp) caster sugar |
| 1 small lime |
| 150 ml (5 fl oz) double cream |
| 2.5 ml (½ tsp) powdered gelatine |
| grated lime rind, to decorate |

**1** Break up the chocolate and place in a small bowl over a pan of simmering water. Gently stir occasionally until it melts to a smooth consistency. Remove from heat and cool slightly.

**2** Place the egg yolks in a deep bowl with the sugar and finely grated lime rind. Whisk with an electric whisk until thick and mousse-like. Whisk in chocolate, then 30 ml (2 tbsp) cream.

**3** Spoon the strained lime juice into a small basin and sprinkle over the gelatine. Leave to soak for about 10 minutes, or until sponge-like in texture. Dissolve by standing the bowl in a pan of simmering water until the gelatine clears and liquefies; whisk into the chocolate mixture.

**4** Finally, whisk the egg whites until stiff but not dry and fold into the chocolate mixture. Divide between two glasses and refrigerate to set. Decorate with a little whipped cream and grated lime rind. Leave at cool room temperature for about 30 minutes before serving.

# Baked Alaska

### SERVES 6–8
*Preparation time: 30 minutes plus 2 hours standing*
*Cooking time: 5 minutes*

| |
|---|
| 225 g (8 oz) fresh or frozen raspberries |
| 30 ml (2 tbsp) orange-flavoured liqueur |
| 20.5 cm (8 inch) cooked sponge flan case |
| 4 egg whites, at room temperature |
| 175 g (6 oz) caster sugar |
| 500 ml (17 fl oz) block vanilla ice cream |

**1** Place the fresh or frozen raspberries on a shallow dish and sprinkle over the liqueur. Cover and leave to macerate for 2 hours, turning occasionally.

**2** Place the sponge flan on a large ovenproof serving dish and spoon the raspberries and juice into the centre.

**3** Whisk the 4 egg whites in a clean, dry bowl until stiff, but not dry. Add 20 ml (4 tsp) caster sugar and whisk again, keeping the mixture stiff. Sprinkle over the remaining sugar and fold through gently.

**4** Fit a piping bag with a large star nozzle and fill with the meringue mixture.

**5** Place the block of ice cream on top of the raspberries, then immediately pipe the meringue on top. Start from the sponge base and pipe the meringue around and over the ice cream until it is completely covered, leaving no gaps.

**6** Immediately place the completed Alaska in a preheated oven and bake at 230°C (450°F) mark 8 for 3–4 minutes. At this stage the meringue should be nicely tinged with brown. Watch the meringue carefully as it burns easily. Do not overcook or the ice cream will become too soft. Serve at once, before the ice cream begins to melt.

# Chapter 8

# *BAKING*

# APPLE GINGERBREAD

**MAKES 12 SLICES**
*Preparation time: 20 minutes*
*Cooking time: 1 hour 30 minutes*

| |
|---|
| 225 g (8 oz) plain flour |
| 2.5 ml (½ tsp) salt |
| 15 ml (1 tbsp) ground ginger |
| 7.5 ml (1½ tsp) baking powder |
| 7.5 ml (1½ tsp) bicarbonate of soda |
| 100 g (4 oz) demerara sugar |
| 75 g (3 oz) butter or Clover |
| 75 g (3 oz) black treacle |
| 75 g (3 oz) golden syrup |
| 150 ml (¼ pint) milk |
| 1 small egg, beaten |
| 1 eating apple, cored and roughly chopped |

**1** Grease and line a 900 g (2 lb) loaf tin. Sift the plain flour into a large bowl with the salt, ginger, baking powder and bicarbonate of soda.

**2** Put the sugar, butter or Clover, treacle and syrup in a saucepan and warm gently over low heat until melted and well blended. Do not allow the mixture to boil. Remove from the heat and leave to cool slightly, until you can hold your hand comfortably against the side of the pan.

**3** Mix in the milk and egg. Make a well in the centre of the dry ingredients, pour in the liquid and mix very thoroughly. Stir in the chopped apple.

**4** Turn into the tin and bake in the oven at 170°C (325°F) mark 3 for about 1½ hours, or until firm to the touch.

**5** Turn out on to a wire rack to cool for at least 1 hour. Wrap in foil, then store in an airtight container for at least 2–3 days before eating.

# CHOCOLATE BRAZIL CAKE

**MAKES 8 SLICES**
*Preparation time: 40 minutes plus 1 hour 15 minutes cooling*
*Cooking time: 1 hour 20 minutes*

| |
|---|
| 100 g (4 oz) plus a knob of butter or Clover |
| flour |
| 300 g (11 oz) plain chocolate |
| 100 g (4 oz) caster sugar |
| 4 eggs, separated |
| 30 ml (2 tbsp) cornflour |
| 175 g (6 oz) Brazil nuts, ground in a food processor |
| 100 g (4 oz) icing sugar |
| plain and milk chocolate curls, to decorate |

**1** Grease a 1.7 litre (3 pint) ring tin. Dust with flour.

**2** Break 200 g (7 oz) chocolate into a small bowl. Add 30 ml (2 tbsp) water. Place over a saucepan of gently simmering water until melted. Remove from the heat and stir until smooth.

**3** Cream 100 g (4 oz) of the butter or Clover with the caster sugar until pale and fluffy. Gradually beat in the egg yolks and cornflour. Fold in the chocolate and nuts.

**4** Whisk egg whites until stiff but not dry. Stir one spoonful of egg white into the mixture to loosen it. Gently fold in the remainder. Spoon into the tin.

**5** Bake at 170°C (325°F) mark 3 for about 1 hour 20 minutes or until a skewer inserted into the centre comes out clean. Leave to cool in the tin for 5 minutes before turning out on to a wire rack to finish cooling.

**6** Place the remaining chocolate in a bowl with the knob of butter or Clover and 60 ml (4 tbsp) water. Melt over a saucepan of simmering water as in stage 2. Beat in the sifted icing sugar until smooth. Cool and then refrigerate for about 15 minutes until the consistency of lightly whipped cream.

**7** Place the cake on its rack over a baking sheet. Spread over the chocolate icing until thinly coated. Decorate with curls of chocolate. Leave to set.

# FROSTED COCONUT CAKE

### MAKES 8 SLICES
*Preparation time: 25 minutes*
*Cooking time: 1 hour 15 minutes*

| |
| --- |
| 50 g (2 oz) shelled hazelnuts |
| 225 g (8 oz) butter or Clover |
| 225 g (8 oz) caster sugar |
| 5 eggs, one of them separated |
| 2.5 ml (½ tsp) vanilla flavouring |
| 100 g (4 oz) plain flour |
| 100 g (4 oz) self-raising flour |
| 40 g (1½ oz) desiccated coconut |
| 75 g (3 oz) icing sugar |
| shredded coconut |

1 Grease a 20 cm (8 inch) base measurement spring-release cake tin. Base-line with greaseproof paper and grease the paper.

2 Spread the nuts out on a baking sheet and brown in the oven at 200°C (400°F) mark 6 for 5–10 minutes. Put into a soft tea towel and rub off the skins. Chop the nuts finely.

3 Put the butter or Clover and sugar into a bowl and beat until pale and fluffy. Whisk 4 whole eggs and 1 yolk together and gradually beat into the creamed mixture with the vanilla flavouring.

4 Combine the flours and fold them into the mixture with 25 g (1 oz) desiccated coconut, and half the nuts.

5 Turn the mixture into the prepared tin and bake in the oven at 180°C (350°F) mark 4 for 45 minutes.

6 Meanwhile prepare a meringue topping: whisk the egg white until stiff and gradually sift and whisk in the icing sugar, keeping the mixture stiff. Fold in the remaining desiccated coconut and chopped hazelnuts.

7 Spoon the meringue topping on to the cake, after it has cooked for 45 minutes, and scatter with shredded coconut.

8 Return to the oven for 20–30 minutes or until a skewer comes out of the cake clean. Check after 15 minutes and cover with a layer of greaseproof paper if it is over-browning. Leave to cool completely for 1 hour.

# APRICOT CRUNCH

### MAKES 16 WEDGES
*Preparation time: 1 hour 20 minutes*
*Cooking time: 35 minutes*

| |
| --- |
| 75 g (3 oz) dried apricots |
| 200 ml (⅓ pint) water |
| 100 g (4 oz) butter or Clover |
| 100 g (4 oz) demerara sugar |
| 75 ml (5 tbsp) golden syrup |
| 200 g (7 oz) crunchy toasted muesli cereal |
| 140 g (5 oz) rolled oats |
| 2.5 ml (½ tsp) mixed spice |
| 10 ml (2 tsp) lemon juice |

1 Base-line two 18 cm (7 inch) round sandwich tins with non-stick paper.

2 Simmer the apricots gently in the water for about 10 minutes, or until softened. Blend contents of pan to form a smooth purée. Cool for about 1 hour.

3 Slowly melt the butter or Clover, sugar and syrup. Stir in the cereal and oats and continue stirring until thoroughly combined. Add the puréed apricots, mixed spice and lemon juice. Mix well.

4 Divide the mixture between the prepared tins and spread evenly over the base. Press down well to level the surface.

5 Bake in the oven at 180°C (350°F) mark 4 for about 35 minutes. Cut each round into eight wedges. Cool in the tin for 30 minutes until firm. Carefully ease the wedges out of the tin and store in an airtight container when completely cold.

# ORANGE MADEIRA CAKE

**MAKES 8 SLICES**
*Preparation time: 20 minutes*
*Cooking time: 60 minutes*

| |
|---|
| 100 g (4 oz) plain flour |
| 100 g (4 oz) self-raising flour |
| 175 g (6 oz) butter or Clover |
| 175 g (6 oz) caster sugar |
| finely grated rind of 2 oranges |
| 5 ml (1 tsp) vanilla flavouring |
| 3 eggs, beaten |
| 15–30 ml (1–2 tbsp) milk (optional) |
| 2–3 thin slices citron peel |

**1** Grease and line an 18 cm (7 inch) round cake tin with greaseproof paper.

**2** Sift the flours together. Cream the butter or Clover, sugar and orange rind until pale and fluffy, then beat in the vanilla flavouring. Add the eggs, a little at a time, beating well after each addition.

**3** Fold in the sifted flours with a metal spoon, adding a little milk if necessary to give a dropping consistency.

**4** Turn the mixture into the tin and bake in the oven at 180°C (350°F) mark 4 for 20 minutes.

**5** Lay the citron peel on top of the cake, return it to the oven and bake for a further 40 minutes until firm. Turn out and cool on a wire rack.

# FRUIT CRUSTED CIDER CAKE

**MAKES 8 SLICES**
*Preparation time: 20 minutes*
*Cooking time: 45–50 minutes*

| |
|---|
| 45 ml (3 tbsp) golden syrup |
| 150 g (5 oz) butter or Clover |
| 350 g (12 oz) cooking apples, peeled, cored and finely chopped |
| 45 ml (3 tbsp) mincemeat |
| 50 g (2 oz) cornflakes, crushed |
| 100 g (4 oz) caster sugar |
| 2 eggs, beaten |
| 100 g (4 oz) self-raising flour |
| 45 ml (3 tbsp) dry cider |

**1** Line a 35.5 × 11.5 cm (14 × 4½ inch) shallow rectangular tart frame with foil. Grease the foil. Put the syrup into a pan with 25 g (1 oz) butter or Clover and melt. Add apples, mincemeat and cornflakes. Set aside.

**2** Put the remaining butter or Clover and the sugar in a bowl and beat together until pale and fluffy. Gradually beat in the eggs.

**3** Fold the flour into the mixture. Pour in the cider and mix it in. Turn the mixture into the prepared frame and level the surface. Spread the apple mixture evenly over it.

**4** Bake in the oven at 170°C (325°F) mark 3 for 45–50 minutes or until firm to the touch. Cool in the metal frame for 1 hour, then cut into bars for serving.

# LEMON CRUMB DROPS

**MAKES ABOUT 36 SMALL CAKES OR
24 LARGER BUNS**
*Preparation time: 20 minutes*
*Cooking time: 20 minutes*

| |
|---|
| 250 g (9 oz) plain white flour |
| 175 g (6 oz) caster sugar |
| pinch salt |
| 100 g (4 oz) butter or Clover |
| 7.5 ml (1½ tsp) baking powder |
| grated rind of 2 lemons |
| 1 egg, beaten |
| 100 ml (4 fl oz) milk |
| 10 ml (2 tsp) light soft brown sugar |
| white vegetable fat |

**1** Rub together 175 g (6 oz) flour, the sugar and salt with 75 g (3 oz) butter or Clover. Reserve one quarter of the mixture.

**2** Add the baking powder to the remaining mixture. Make a well in the centre and add the lemon rind, egg and milk. Beat with a wooden spoon, gradually incorporating the dry ingredients until the mixture forms a smooth batter.

**3** Rub the brown sugar, remaining flour and butter or Clover into the reserved crumb mixture.

**4** Lightly brush a mini cup-cake sheet with the melted vegetable fat or arrange 24 paper cake cases in two 12-hole bun tins. Spoon a little of the cake batter into each 'cup' and sprinkle with the crumb mix.

**5** Bake at 190°C (375°F) mark 5 for 15–20 minutes for the smaller cakes and 25 minutes for the larger cakes, or until well risen and golden. Cool on a wire rack. If using the mini cup-cake sheet, repeat with any remaining mixture, brushing the cup-cake sheet lightly with the melted fat between each batch.

*Left: Lemon Crumb Drops*

# SPICED WALNUT SCONES

**MAKES 16**
*Preparation time: 15 minutes*
*Cooking time: 18 minutes*

| |
|---|
| 100 g (4 oz) plain wholemeal flour |
| 100 g (4 oz) plain white flour |
| 15 ml (3 tsp) baking powder |
| 2.5 ml (½ tsp) ground mixed spice |
| pinch of salt |
| 50 g (2 oz) butter or Clover |
| 15 ml (1 tbsp) caster sugar |
| 75 g (3 oz) walnut pieces, roughly chopped |
| 10 ml (2 tsp) lemon juice |
| 200 ml (7 fl oz) milk |
| chopped walnuts and honey, to decorate |

**1** Sift the flours into a bowl with the baking powder, mixed spice and salt. Stir in the bran (from the wholemeal flour) left in the bottom of the sieve. Rub in the butter or Clover. Stir in the sugar and two-thirds of the walnuts.

**2** Mix the lemon juice with 170 ml (6 fl oz) of the milk and stir into the dry ingredients until evenly mixed.

**3** Turn the dough onto a floured surface and knead lightly until smooth and soft.

**4** Roll out the dough to a 20.5 cm (8 inch) square and place on a baking sheet. Mark the surface into 16 squares, cutting the dough through to a depth of 3 mm (⅛ inch).

**5** Lightly brush the dough with the remaining milk, then sprinkle over the remaining chopped walnut pieces.

**6** Bake in the oven at 220°C (425°F) mark 7 for about 18 minutes or until well risen, golden brown and firm to the touch. Cut into squares. Serve warm, brushed with honey.

# MUESLI BISCUITS

**MAKES ABOUT 18**
*Preparation time: 15 minutes*
*Cooking time: 15 minutes*

| |
|---|
| 100 g (4 oz) butter or Clover |
| 50 g (2 oz) demerara sugar |
| 15 ml (1 tbsp) honey |
| 50 g (2 oz) self-raising wholemeal flour |
| 225 g (8 oz) unsweetened muesli |
| 1 egg |

**1** Cream together the butter or Clover and sugar. Mix in the remaining ingredients to form a firm dough.

**2** Roll the dough into smooth balls the size of walnuts. Place well apart on a greased baking sheet and flatten slightly with the palm of the hand.

**3** Bake in the oven at 190°C (375°F) mark 5 for 15 minutes or until crisp and golden brown. Leave to cool on a wire rack.

# SHORTBREAD FINGERS

**MAKES ABOUT 18**
*Preparation time: 20 minutes*
*Cooking time: 15 minutes*

| |
|---|
| 100 g (4 oz) butter or Clover |
| 50 g (2 oz) caster sugar |
| 100 g (4 oz) plain flour |
| 50 g (2 oz) ground rice |
| caster sugar, to dredge |

**1** In a bowl, cream the butter or Clover until soft. Add the caster sugar and beat until pale and fluffy.

**2** Add the flour and ground rice and stir until the mixture binds together. Knead well to form a smooth dough.

**3** Roll out the dough on a lightly floured surface, to a square about 1 cm (½ inch) thick. Cut the square in half then cut each into fingers about 2 cm (¾ inch) wide.

**4** Place the fingers well apart on a baking sheet and prick them with a fork. Bake in the oven at 180°C (350°F) mark 4 for about 15 minutes, or until pale golden brown and just firm to the touch.

**5** Transfer to a wire rack and leave to cool for 5 minutes. Dredge with caster sugar, then allow to cool completely for about 30 minutes.

# CHEWY CHOCOLATE BROWNIES

**MAKES 16**
*Preparation time: 10 minutes*
*Cooking time: 25 minutes*

| |
|---|
| 75 g (3 oz) plain flour |
| 175 g (6 oz) dark soft brown sugar |
| 25 g (1 oz) cocoa powder |
| 1.25 ml (¼ tsp) salt |
| 100 g (4 oz) butter or Clover |
| 2 eggs, beaten |
| 5 ml (1 tsp) vanilla flavouring |
| 75 g (3 oz) chopped mixed nuts |

**1** Put all the ingredients in a bowl and beat thoroughly (preferably with an electric whisk) until evenly combined.

**2** Turn the mixture into a greased 20.5 cm (8 inch) square cake and level the surface with a palette knife.

**3** Bake in the oven at 180°C (350°F) mark 4 for 25 minutes until only just set (the mixture should still wobble slightly in the centre). Stand the cake tin on a wire rack and leave until the cake is completely cold. Cut into 16 squares and put in an airtight tin.

# CHOCOLATE VIENNESE FINGERS

**MAKES ABOUT 18**
*Preparation time: 30 minutes plus 30 minutes cooling*
*Cooking time: 20 minutes*

| |
|---|
| 100 g (4 oz) butter or Clover |
| 25 g (1 oz) icing sugar |
| 75 g (3 oz) plain chocolate |
| 100 g (4 oz) plain flour |
| 1.25 ml (¼ tsp) baking powder |
| 15 ml (1 tbsp) drinking chocolate powder |
| vanilla flavouring |

**1** Grease two baking sheets. Put the butter or Clover into a bowl and beat until pale and soft, then beat in the icing sugar.

**2** Break 25 g (1 oz) chocolate into a heatproof bowl and place over simmering water. Stir until the chocolate is melted, then remove from heat and leave to cool for 10 minutes.

**3** When the chocolate is cool, but not thick, beat it into the creamed mixture.

**4** Sift in the flour, baking powder and drinking chocolate. Beat well, adding a few drops of vanilla flavouring.

**5** Spoon into a piping bag fitted with a medium star nozzle and pipe finger shapes about 7.5 cm (3 inches) long on to the prepared baking sheets, allowing room between each for the mixture to spread. Bake at 190°C (375°F) mark 5 for 15–20 minutes until crisp and pale golden. Cool on a wire rack for 30 minutes.

**6** When the fingers are cold, break the remaining 50 g (2 oz) chocolate into a heatproof bowl. Stand the bowl over a pan of simmering water and stir until the chocolate has melted. Remove from the heat and dip both ends of the fingers into the melted chocolate. Leave on a wire rack for 30 minutes to set.

*Left: Mixed Fruit Teabread (page 94)*
*Right: Chocolate Brazil Cake (page 85)*

# MIXED FRUIT TEABREAD

### SERVES 8
*Preparation time: 15 minutes plus overnight soaking*
*Cooking time: 1 hour 30 minutes*

| |
|---|
| 175 g (6 oz) raisins |
| 100 g (4 oz) sultanas |
| 50 g (2 oz) currants |
| 100 g (4 oz) light brown soft sugar |
| 300 ml (½ pint) cold tea |
| 1 egg, beaten |
| 45 ml (3 tbsp) golden syrup |
| 225 g (8 oz) plain wholemeal flour |
| 7.5 ml (1½ tsp) baking powder |
| 2.5 ml (½ tsp) mixed spice |

**1** Soak the dried fruit and sugar in the tea overnight. Grease and base-line a 1.6 litre (2¾ pint) loaf tin.

**2** Beat the egg and syrup into the fruit mixture. Add the flour, baking powder and spice and mix well. Spoon into the prepared tin.

**3** Bake in the oven at 170°C (325°F) mark 3 for 30 minutes. Cover loosely with foil and cook for 40–60 minutes until well risen and just firm. Turn on to a wire rack to cool. Wrap in foil, and eat after 1–2 days.

# DATE AND RAISIN TEABREAD

### SERVES 6–8
*Preparation time: 20 minutes*
*Cooking time: 1 hour 15 minutes*

| |
|---|
| 100 g (4 oz) butter or Clover |
| 275 g (10 oz) plain flour, sifted |
| 100 g (4 oz) stoned dates, chopped |
| 50 g (2 oz) walnut halves, chopped |
| 100 g (4 oz) seedless raisins |
| 100 g (4 oz) golden syrup |
| 5 ml (1 tsp) baking powder |
| 5 ml (1 tsp) bicarbonate of soda |
| 150 ml (¼ pint) milk |

**1** Grease and line a loaf tin measuring 25 × 15 cm (9¾ × 5¾ inches). Rub the butter or Clover into the flour and stir in the dates, walnuts, raisins and syrup.

**2** Mix the baking powder, bicarbonate of soda and milk and pour into the dry ingredients; mix to give a stiff dropping consistency.

**3** Turn the mixture into the tin and bake in the oven at 170°C (325°F) mark 3 for about 30 minutes. Cover loosely with foil and cook for 45 minutes, until well risen and just firm to the touch. Turn out and cool on a wire rack.

# INDEX

Almond beef with celery  40
Apple gingerbread  85
Apricot crunch  86
Artichoke:
   Jerusalem artichokes in mustard
     sauce  67
   Prawn and artichoke salad  13
Asparagus tartlets  16
Aubergine:
   Aubergine and pepper salad  67
   Stuffed aubergines  20
Avocado:
   Baked avocados and
     mushrooms  17

Baked Alaska  83
Beef:
   Almond beef with celery  40
   Gingered beef casserole  36
   Stilton steaks  36
Biscuits:
   Chocolate Viennese fingers  91
   Muesli biscuits  90
   Shortbread fingers  90
Bread and butter pudding  79

Cabbage:
   Red cabbage and garlic  66
   Stir-fried cabbage with walnuts  66
Cakes:
   Apple gingerbread  85
   Apricot crunch  86
   Chewy chocolate brownies  91
   Chocolate brazil cake  85
   Frosted coconut cake  86
   Fruit crusted cider cake  87
   Lemon crumb drops  89
   Orange madeira cake  87

Chicken:
   Chicken liver bolognese  45
   Chicken liver and mushroom
     salad  24
   Chicken paprikash  44
   Chicken with tarragon sauce  45
   Chicken waterzooi  10
   Parsley chicken with cashew  44
   Spanish chicken and rice  48
   Stoved chicken  48
Chocolate:
   Chewy chocolate brownies  91
   Chocolate brazil cake  85
   Chocolate coffee refrigerator
     slice  82
   Chocolate and lime mousse  83
   Chocolate Viennese fingers  91
   Hot chocolate cheesecake  82
Coconut:
   Frosted coconut cake  86
   Steamed coconut sponge with
     orange custard  78
Cod:
   Stuffed cod crêpes  63
Cream of watercress and cheese
   soup  12
Curried parsnip and apple soup  10

Date and raisin teabread  94
Desserts:
   Baked Alaska  83
   Chocolate coffee refrigerator
     slice  82
   Chocolate and lime mousse  83
   Glazed nut flan  75
   Hot chocolate cheesecake  82
   Meringue basket  79
   Raspberry walnut torte  74
   Spiced bread and butter
     pudding  79

Steamed coconut sponge with
   orange custard  78
Strawberry custard tart  78
Walnut pear slice  74
Duck:
   Duckling with green peas  51
   Sweet and sour duck  51

Egg:
   Pepper and tomato omelette  28
   Smoked haddock scramble  21
   Spicy Scotch eggs  25
Escalopes with herbs  37

Fettuccine in creamy ham and
   mushroom sauce  24
Fish. *See also individual names*
   Golden fish lasagne  60
   Potato-topped fish pie  59
Frosted coconut cake  86
Fruit crusted cider cake  86
Fruit teabread  94

Gingerbread, apple  85
Gingered beef casserole  36
Golden fish lasagne  60
Gratin of seafood  55
Gruyère potatoes  70

Haddock:
   Golden fish lasagne  60
   Haddock and corn chowder  16
   Smoked haddock scramble  21
Halibut with wine and tomatoes  58
Honeyed lamb noisettes  32

95

Jerusalem artichokes in mustard
    sauce 67

Lamb:
    Honeyed lamb noisettes 32
    Lamb and rosemary pilaff 30
    Minted lamb grill 30
Lemon crumb drops 89
Liver and bacon with potato
    pancakes 41

Macaroni pie 21
Mackerel fillets in oatmeal and
    almonds 55
Meringue basket 79
Minestrone 12
Minted lamb grill 30
Muesli biscuits 90
Mushroom:
    Mushroom and ham risotto 70
    Sesame mushrooms 66
Mussels in tomato sauce 59

Nut flan, glazed 75

Orange madeira cake 87

Parsley chicken with cashew 44
Parsnip:
    Curried parsnip and apple soup 10
    Parsnip croquettes 65
Pear:
    Walnut pear slice 74
Pepper and tomato omelette 28
Pissaladière 25
Pizza casalinga 20

Plaice:
    Poached plaice and spinach flan 62
Pork:
    Pork escalopes with sage 40
    Pork fillet with white wine and
        mushrooms 32
    Pork steaks with peppers 33
    Pork and vegetable stir fry 33
Potato:
    Gruyère potatoes 70
    Potato pancakes 41
    Potato-topped fish pie 59
    Red flannel hash 28
Prawn and artichoke salad 13

Raspberry walnut torte 74
Red cabbage and garlic 66
Red flannel hash 28
Rice:
    Lamb and rosemary pilaff 30
    Mushroom and ham risotto 70
    Spanish chicken and rice 48

Salad niçoise 63
Salmon fillet en croûte 58
Scones, spiced walnut 89
Scotch eggs, spicy 25
Seafood, gratin of 55
Seafood salad, Italian 13
Sesame mushrooms 66
Shortbread fingers 90
Skate with capers 62
Smoked haddock scramble 21
Smoked trout and apple mousse 17
Soup:
    Chicken waterzooi 10
    Cream of watercress and cheese
        soup 12
    Curried parsnip and apple soup 10
    Haddock and corn chowder 16
    Minestrone 12
Spanish chicken and rice 48
Spiced bread and butter pudding 79

Spicy Scotch eggs 25
Starters: See also Soup
    Asparagus tartlets 16
    Baked avocado and
        mushrooms 17
    Prawn and artichoke salad 13
    Seafood salad, Italian 13
    Smoked trout and apple
        mousse 17
Stilton steaks 36
Stoved chicken 48
Strawberry custard tart 78
Stuffed aubergines 20
Stuffed cod crêpes 63
Summer pasta 24
Summer vegetable fricassée 65
Sweet and sour duck 51

Teabreads 94
Trout:
    Smoked trout and apple
        mousse 17
    Trout poached in wine 60
Turkey:
    Turkey puff pie 50
    Turkey in spiced yogurt 50

Veal:
    Escalopes with herbs 37
    Pan-fried veal with mustard and
        cream 37

Walnut:
    Raspberry walnut torte 74
    Spiced walnut scones 89
    Stir-fried cabbage with walnuts 66
    Walnut pear slice 74
Watercress:
    Cream of watercress and cheese
        soup 12